The Great Tapestry of Scotland

THE GREAT TAPESTRY OF SCOTLAND

PANEL I

The Great Tapestry of Scotland

Alistair Moffat

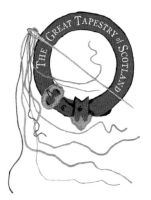

BIRLINN

For all those who have worked on The Great Tapestry of Scotland

**Panel 1 on page ii
stitched by:**

KA Two

Linda McClarkin
Carol Whiteford

Stitched in:
Beith, Kilwinning

**Panel 158 on page xvi
stitched by:**

The Red Lichties

Evelyn Chaplain
Bob Chaplain
Rena Freeburn
Janette Nairn
Eileen Shepherd
Alice Sim
Jessy Smart
Mary Stephen
Linda Walker
Margaret Wynne

Stitched in:
Inverkeilor, Arbroath

First published in 2013 by
Birlinn Limited
West Newington House
10 Newington Road
Edinburgh EH9 1QS

www.birlinn.co.uk

2

ISBN: 978 1 78027 160 6

British Library Cataloguing-in-Publication Data
A catalogue record for this book is available from the British Library

Typeset by Mark Blackadder

Printed and bound by Hussar Books, Poland

Foreword

The tapestry illustrated in this book tells the story of Scotland. As one might imagine, to illustrate the history of a country, even with some 165 panels at one's disposal, is no easy task. Nor is it easy to tell it in a way that brings centuries of a nation's existence to life in an entertaining and vivid way. The Great Tapestry of Scotland does all this, and it does it in a way that was instantly recognised and appreciated by the public when it first went on show in the Scottish Parliament in the late summer of 2013. People came in their thousands – so many, in fact, that at times the building was thought to have reached capacity and faced the hitherto unthought-of possibility of being closed for a few hours.

I was part of the group of people behind the tapestry project, and I went to the opening with my heart in my mouth. What would the public judgement be on a project that had such large ambitions? Would people find fault with our selection of subjects? Would the artist's style fail to resonate with the people of Scotland? I need not have worried for a moment on any of these scores. People stood before the tapestry with wonderment and delight on their faces. Some cried with emotion – the greatest tribute, I think, that any work of art can be given. I saw young children gazing at the panels with rapt attention. I saw elderly people recognise images and references and share them with each other with all the joy that goes with discovering something one has long known about but perhaps forgotten or not thought about for a long time. Everybody standing before the tapestry seemed transported by the experience.

The tapestry is the work of more than a thousand people from all over Scotland and beyond. The central artistic vision, though, is that of three people: Alistair Moffat, who selected the subject matter and wrote the text; Andrew Crummy, who drew the designs; and Dorie Wilkie, who supervised and inspired the stitching. All three made this object, but Andrew is the one who must be particularly celebrated as the artist. A man of great modesty, he never seeks praise, but it must be said here that he has, quite simply, wrought a masterpiece.

Then there are the many stitchers who have themselves put their own artistic stamp on the tapestry. Although Andrew designed the main images, he generously left a great deal of scope for individual stitchers to make their own contribution. And they have done so magnificently, adding numerous touches throughout, giving yet more life and colour to this lovely object.

When we started this project, which began with a telephone call I made to Andrew Crummy proposing that we do it, I had no idea that the result would be so lovely and so affecting. I had no idea, too, that in bringing the tapestry to completion so many people would be brought together in friendship. But that has all happened, and now the Scottish nation has something that it can treasure for many years – centuries, we hope – to remind us all of who we are and all the love, suffering, hope, disappointment, and triumph that makes up the life of a people. I hope, too, that we shall be able to share that with others from other nations, who will see the universal human story written on these panels of linen and perhaps reflect on the ideals of brother- and sisterhood that have always been so important in Scotland and remain so today.

Alexander McCall Smith

Introduction

On a summer afternoon in the 1890s, Donald MacIver drove his pony and trap up the track on the west side of Loch Roag on the Atlantic shore of the Isle of Lewis. A teacher at the school at Breascleit, he found himself completing the last stage of a long journey back into the past. Beside Donald sat an old man. His uncle, Domnhall Ban Crosd, had sailed across the ocean from Canada so that, before he died, he could at last return home. As Donald flicked the reins and the pony trotted up the rise at Miabhig, the vast panorama of the mighty Atlantic opened before them. Below spread the pale yellow sands of Uig at low tide and around the bay lay a scatter of townships.

His by-names hint at Domnhall Ban's demeanour. Common enough when used to distinguish the owner of a frequently found name, *ban* means 'fair headed' but *crosd* is unusual – probably deriving from an English adjective, it is somewhere between 'obstinate' and 'ill natured'. Perhaps the old man set a characteristic stone-face when he gazed on the heartbreakingly beautiful bay at Uig, the water glinting in the summer sun, a sparkle, a sight he had not beheld for fifty years, not since the white-sailed ships slipped over the horizon bound for a new life in Canada.

As Donald guided his pony gently over the rutted tracks, grass growing green on their crests, they came at last to journey's end, the place Domnhall Ban Crosd had seen only in his dreams. It was the township of Carnais, his birthplace, where crofting families had been cleared off the land by the agents of an absent and uncaring aristocracy in 1851. Like many, Domnhall Ban and his people had found good and even prosperous lives in Canada but, in their hearts, there was *ionndrainn*. It means 'something that is missing', 'an emptiness', and, before he grew too old for a long sea voyage, the child of Carnais wanted to see his home place once more. But, when Donald pulled on the reins and braked the trap, there was nothing. Nothing at all to see. The croft houses had been tumbled down, the fences and fields opened to sheep pasture. What had been a busy, living landscape, home to the chatter of children and the day-in, day-out labour of farming families, had simply been obliterated. As he looked around at the desolation, the old man's face at last crumpled and he wept, tears falling for all that experience in one place, all lost and gone, memories that would die with him. '*Chaneil nith an seo mar a bha e, ach an ataireachd na mara,*' he said to his nephew – 'There is nothing here now as it was, except for the surge of the sea.'

Much moved by his uncle's sadness, Donald MacIver wrote his great lyric, '*An Ataireachd Ard*'. In memory of loss and change, of the wash of history over Scotland, it begins:

> *An ataireachd bhuan*
> *Cluinn fuaim na h'ataireachd ard*
> *That torunn a'chuain*
> *Mar chualas leams' e 'nam phaisd*
> *Gun mhuthadh, gun truas*
> *A' sluaisreadh gainneimh na tragh'd*
> *An ataireachd bhuan*
> *Cluinn fuaim na h'ataireachd ard.*

The ceaseless surge
Listen to the surge of the sea
The thunder of the ocean
As I heard it when I was a child
Without change, without pity
Breaking on the sands of the beach
The ceaseless surge
Listen to the surge of the sea.

The Great Tapestry of Scotland begins and ends with images of the ceaseless surge of the sea. The thunder of the ocean, its belly-hollowing elemental beauty is where our story of Scotland begins and it may well be where it ends, aeons into the future. But what made the rhythm and swirl of Donald MacIver's words resonate was his uncle's grief at the unflinching passage of time and the destruction of the way of life of ordinary people. And despite his tears, the old man's instinctive understanding that it could not be other. Lying on the edge of beyond, the land of Scotland, the hard, ancient rocks of Lewisian gneiss, the old red sandstone and the shales and coal of the Midland Valley, endure but the story of the people who lived on its straths, in its river valleys and glens changes constantly and sometimes brutally.

No mere backdrop, Scotland is utterly singular. Most who see a photograph or a sequence on TV of a landscape without road signs or a familiar landmark can recognise it instantly and intuitively as a place in Scotland. Not sure exactly where but it's definitely Scotland. There is a mixture of atmosphere, look and something very simple. The colours of Scotland are like no other and, above all, the Great Tapestry and its thousand makers have perfectly captured the blues, greens, reds, greys and browns of our distinctive geography.

The sorrow of Domnhall Ban Crosd is also characteristic. The old man did not weep for the passing of empires, the boasts of Ozymandias, he did not stand in the magnificent ruins of greatness, he wept for the scatter of once-snug cottage walls, for the passing of a way of life, for the body-warmth of a dying culture, the humanity of shared ills and privations, the clear and unambiguous sense of a community, the ghosts of people who would help each other when the waves crashed on Mangersta Head and storms blew in off the ocean. On that summer afternoon, Domnhall Ban knew that night had fallen on Carnais.

If those who look at its panels also listen closely to the Great Tapestry, they will hear something of what it sounds like, not only like the thunder of the ocean but also the distant march of armies, the jingle of harness, the roar of cannon and the echo of oratory. But much louder and more insistent will be the tread of ordinary people, the *craic* by the fireside, the whispers of hunters in the wildwood, the chatter of plough teams, the whistle of a shepherd, the clatter and rattle of mills, foundries and shipyards. And the singing, the waulking songs, the pawky melodies of Harry Lauder, the psalms, the keening and the grief. The sounds of a community, what Domnhall Ban knew at Carnais. But, despite the efforts of the powerful, the disengaged and outsiders, Scotland is still, just, a community, and a series of connected communities. Scots still believe in a collective sense of ourselves and that society should take responsibility for the old, the weak and the poor. Lest this sound like a manifesto, it should be pointed out that it is not a proposal for the future but an observation of what happened in the past – and in the present. The Great Tapestry is, after all, the creation of a community – the thousand stitchers who came together in groups to make it.

And, lest our sense of ourselves becomes self-congratulatory, the ceaseless surge of the sea and the ungraspable millions of years it took to form the geology of our nation remind us that the history of Scotland is but a speck bobbing on the ocean of time. Eleven thousand years may seem like an epic sweep but it is as nothing when the night sky is clear and the light of dead stars shines down on our tiny planet. And, being Scots, we should be further chastened by the knowledge that, if we have somehow managed to retain a worthwhile, workable sense of community, there were plenty of times when we behaved extremely badly and continue to.

The Great Tapestry of Scotland is, then, a people's history of a people, made by a thousand of those people. That says much about its content, its cultural bent, but why exactly is it so beautiful, so evocative and how did it come into being?

Alexander McCall Smith is the simple answer to the last question. He made it happen. Having seen the remarkable Prestonpans Tapestry, a beautiful embroidered record of the battle fought near the town in 1745, Sandy was impressed not only with the panels and their design but also with the impact they had on those who looked at them. They were mesmerised. An idea leapt into Sandy's head. Why not make a tapestry that tells all of Scotland's story and do it for 2014, the Year of Homecoming, the Commonwealth Games in Glasgow, the Ryder Cup at Gleneagles, the 700th anniversary of Bannockburn? A tapestry of Scotland for Scotland's year. The artistic inspiration behind the Prestonpans project was Andrew Crummy and, once Sergeant McCall Smith had recruited him, he called me. What should be in it? How should the narrative run? Would I write it? Within ten seconds, I was enlisted – Corporal Moffat, sir. Our platoon was completed when Dorie Wilkie, the wonderful Head Stitcher on the Prestonpans Tapestry, agreed to oversee the making of what we decided to call The Great Tapestry of Scotland. Gillian Harte became our excellent administrator and, finally and vitally, Jan Rutherford and Anna Renz agreed to do the publicity and raise the funds needed. They did a superb job.

Now we needed an army, a thousand volunteer stitchers to transform my narrative and Andrew Crummy's superb drawings into the tapestry. And, once the call went out, they enlisted within months. Groups of stitchers sat down all over Scotland, from Shetland to Galloway, and they began the hard, detailed, fiddly, inspiring work of making all come alive.

Principal amongst the pleasures of working on this unique project has been my collaboration with Andrew Crummy. In the best Scottish tradition, I kent his mother – the remarkable Helen Crummy who founded the Craigmillar Festival Society – and, with his passionate inherited interest in community arts, Andrew is certainly his mother's son. From the outset, we agreed that if the tapestry was to speak clearly of Scotland, then it had to tell a story of our people, of all who lived here for all those who live here now.

What made collaboration a joy was Andrew's abundant talent. He knows how to make bold statements, his drawing is absolutely assured and it proceeds from a clear grasp of the essential narrative. No messing about, arrow-straight to the point. The lyrical opening panel shows Andrew's talent perfectly as sheep, fish and birds dance in the hair of the woman who looks up at the hand with the needle while, around her, the arms of others enfold scenes and objects of Scotland – standing stones, tenements, shipyards, books, musical instruments and a football. And, moving briskly through the picture plane, trains puff across viaducts, ships sail, fully rigged, to unknown destinations while an oil drilling platform is planted in the sea. It is nothing less than the singular, all-encompassing, wholly original work of a great artist.

Crucially, Andrew also understood what stitchers liked to stitch and his drawings deliberately involved them directly in the creative process, inviting them to add images, even alter the original. We both talked of Renaissance altarpieces and how painters appended predella panels below the Virgin and Child, the Crucifixion or the Adoration of the Magi or whatever the main image was. In these, painters sometimes added street scenes, landscapes or a portrait of the donor and, by leaving spaces in the drawings, Andrew and I hoped that stitchers would take the initiative. And they did! We also hoped that each would attach an impresa and perhaps initials. And they did. They made it their own.

What further encouraged additional bits of history in each panel was geography. Not only did the tapestry have to tell a story of the Scots, it had to include as much of the land of Scotland as was feasible. Panels were set in the Northern Isles, the Highlands, the cities, the Hebrides, the Midland Valley, Galloway and the Borders. And then, very importantly, those linked to a particular area were usually sent to groups of stitchers who lived in the same area. And that process of matching was wonderfully fruitful.

The needs of a wide geographical spread did not inhibit my major task – what to include and what to exclude. Over the eleven millennia of our story, Scotland has changed enormously. Cities did not always exist and places now sparsely populated were once important. Before 3,000 BC, very few hunter-gatherers lived in the wildwood and it seems that the islands of the Atlantic coast supported a much larger proportion of the population than they do now. Before 1700, the vast majority of Scots lived in the countryside while after 1900 most had moved to the Lowland cities. Without bending the narrative out of shape, it was possible to locate Scotland's story right across the nation.

Drama is naturally eye-catching and it would have been easy to arrange our past around a series of battles, wars, martyrdoms and coronations and the other familiar set pieces. And some did insist on inclusion. But, generally, it seemed better to talk of how change affected the many rather than leaders or elites of various sorts. For those who worked the land for generations, invasion and political change often meant the replacement of one set of masters with another. The great problem is silence. Written records usually noted the doings of the mighty, the notorious and the saintly – and rarely have anything to say about ordinary people. Andrew and I therefore decided to show something of the lives of the many with generic panels, images of people working, walking their lives under Scotland's huge skies. These are simple and eloquent, needing little explanation.

Early Scotland is also – conventionally – a story of men. My own work in DNA studies and elsewhere has led me to believe that, in the millennia before the last two centuries, the status of women was little better than that of informal slavery. And so Andrew and I took every opportunity to include female figures, wherever figures were needed, both in the specific and generic panels. *Clann-Nighean an Sgadain*, the Hebridean Herring Girls who followed the fishing fleets in the 19th and early 20th centuries to gut and barrel the herring catch as it came ashore around Scotland's ports, is a good example. We did not distort our national story to include women where they were not actors in events, but we recognised that always they were there, giving life to the nation, and we tried never to forget that.

Not that we would have been allowed to. Almost all of the stitchers are women and they would not have let us do anything less. That fact remains an absolutely determinant influence.

The completion of this epic project is also the end of an equally epic, long, emotional and unexpected journey. And the tapestry itself is unexpected. Two years ago, I had no idea that it would look like it does. The Great Tapestry of Scotland sparkles, glows and surprises. It is not only the work of Andrew Crummy, Dorie Wilkie and myself, inspired by Sandy McCall Smith, it is a unique expression – a history of a nation written and made by a thousand people.

OH WIND HAE MAIRCY, HAUD YER WHISHT, FOR I DAURNA LISTEN MAIR!

OH TELL ME FIT WAS ON YER ROAD, YE ROARIN NORLAND WIND?

FAR ABUNE THE ANGUS STRATHS I SAW THE WILD GEESE FLEE

THE INCHCAPE BELL

THE INCHCAPE BELL

PROPTER LIBER TATUM

PANEL 158

The Tapestries

*Almost all of the images and the panels are
easy to understand and some have text to help
identify who is who and what is what. They
also run in a broadly chronological order but
what follows adds a context, the briefest summary
of the story of Scotland, background music for
this stunning procession of the past.*

PANEL 2 The Ceaseless Sea

Panels stitched by:

Helen Nairn
Frances MacLean
Debbie Muir
Nino Stewart
Marjorie Watters

Stitched in:
Kinlochmoidart

In the beginning was the sea. Hundreds of millions of years ago, when the Earth was very young and vast primordial landmasses rose and were submerged, what would become Scotland was unrecognisable. Different parts of our familiar and beloved geography lay far distant from each other, some were attached to huge continents, some were splintered fragments, still others lay submerged on the bed of an ancient ocean. Lying between three palaeo-continents, Laurentia, Baltica and Avalonia, the great expanse of the Iapetus Ocean was beginning to shrink as tectonic movement shaped and reshaped the crust of the Earth. An unimaginably long time ago, about 410 million years, much of what became Scotland was waiting to rise out of the prehistoric seas and be welded together into one of the most geologically distinct places on our planet. Scotland was to be the deposit of a series of ancient collisions. And, throughout our prehistory and in more modern times, these collisions would remain central to an understanding of our nation and its people. Our history is written in our rocks just as surely as it is in monastic chronicles, census returns or the stones and bones of archaeological digs.

PANEL 3a The Formation of Scotland

Panel stitched by:

North Berwick Creative Embroidery Group

Carole Bailey
Angeniet Black
Audrey Brown
Tertia Crawford
Margaret Dinning
Margaret Holm
Vi Jones
Pat Lucas
Bunty McInroy
Isobel Russell
Margaret Struth
Lyn Vaughan
Sandra Walker

Stitched in:
Dunbar, Gullane,
East Linton, North Berwick

As powerful tectonic forces bulldozed the great continents across the face of the Earth, splinters were sometimes sheared off. Known as terranes, four very different rock formations were ground together to make the map of Scotland. To the north-west, Lewisian gneiss made the Western Isles, Coll, Tiree, Iona, the western peninsula of Islay known as the Rhinns and parts of the Atlantic coastline. Tremendously hard, the gneiss is igneous, forged deep in the molten crust of the Earth and forced upwards as the palaeo-continents moved, buckling and corrugating the strata. To the east and south of the Lewisian formations, thick layers of Old Red Sandstone predominate and their most spectacular monuments are the Torridon Mountains and the singular peak of Suilven. Below the Great Glen lie Dalriadan rocks, mostly strata of sandstone, shale and limestone. The mountains and glens of such as the Cairngorms were moulded and changed as volcanoes roared and ice ages froze the land. Below the abrupt frontier of the Highland Boundary Fault, the geology of the Midland Valley, better known as the Central Belt, was originally formed in tropical latitudes. Many millions of years ago, vast and dense forests grew where Glasgow, Stirling, Perth and Edinburgh now stand. It was swampland and, as the trees died and fell, they made layers of carbon. These strata would much later become Scotland's coalfields. The Southern Upland Fault was formed by the fourth terrane. Following a line from Ballantrae in Ayrshire to Dunbar on the Firth of Forth, its hills were once the bed of a primordial ocean.

PANEL 3b The Collision

Some way to the south of the Southern Upland Fault lies a fascinating geological relic. On the west coast of the Isle of Man, near the hamlet of Niarbyl, the cliffs of a small cove have running diagonally across them a thin, greyish-white seam of rock. It is visible for only a hundred metres or so before it disappears into the waters of the Irish Sea but it is a memorial to the making of Scotland. Known as the Iapetus Suture, it marks the precise place where the vast continents of Laurentia and Avalonia collided, having welded the four terranes together. And as an entertaining footnote, the harder rocks of the Southern Upland Fault caused the strata of the softer rocks of the North of England to buckle and push the coal and iron ore seams nearer to the surface. In this way, Galloway and the Borders made West Cumbria and Tyneside a gift of their traditional industries. The angle of the ancient collision is remembered in the north-east to south-west slant of Scotland's geography, the Great Glen, the Highland Boundary Fault, the Midland Valley and the Southern Upland Fault, to say nothing of the compass direction of the modern border between England and Scotland. The grain of the land has been immensely influential on our history. Upland and lowland follows it, lochs and rivers run that way, tracks and roads are forced to take its direction. Geology formed Scotland and the land and the sea formed the character of the people.

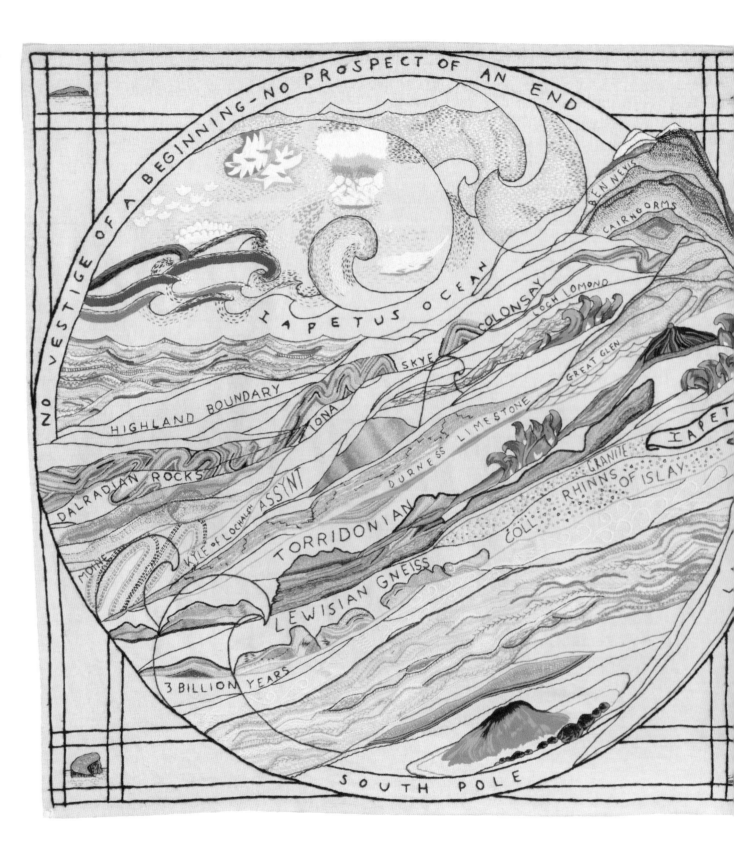

ST KILDA

BEN MORE

AILSA CRAIG

SKYE

NORTH BERWICK

ARTHUR'S SEAT

ARDNAMURCHAN

...TURE

DUMFRIES

GARLETON HILLS

MAUCHLINE

SHALE COAL

DESERT

SALISBURY CRAGS

...NIA

CORAL REEF

SICCAR POINT

SOUTHERN UPLANDS

PANEL 4   Scotland Emerges from the Ice

Panel stitched by:

Pioneer Panelbeaters

Eileen Henderson
Laura Henderson
Annette Hunter
Kirsten Hunter

Stitched in:
Linlithgow, Edinburgh

The last ice age ended very much more recently. Some time around 9,000 BC, glaciers began to groan, splinter and grind over the landscape of Scotland like prehistoric sandpaper. Bulldozing boulders, gravel and other deposits, they shaped familiar landmarks like Stirling and Edinburgh's castle rocks, they scarted out glens and sea lochs, rolling hills and mountains. And, when the ice at last drew back, people came – the Pioneers who first settled Scotland. They came from the south – some from the ice-age refuges, the famous painted caves on either side of the Pyrenees, others walked to Scotland from the east. Until c. 6,000 BC, the southern basin of the North Sea was dry land. What first drew the Pioneers, our earliest ancestors, northwards was probably the migration of the animals they depended on. Many were cold adapted, like reindeer, and, as the ice melted very quickly in a process known as climate flick- ering, the animals could not evolve fast enough and so they were forced to chase the cold. And our ancestors followed them north. Although they looked like us, these hunter-gatherers will have seemed young to a modern eye. Few lived beyond the age of thirty, women perhaps dying young because of complications in childbirth. Since the bone needle had been invented, the Pioneers were able to make warm and close- fitting garments from skins, their look probably most resembling that of the Forest Indians of the eastern United States. When they came to Scotland, they may have come to a land of plenty, a place where roots, fruits, nuts and berries grew and fish and prey animals thrived. And their arrival reminds us of a basic historical truth – every Scot is an immigrant. The only question is when our ancestors arrived.

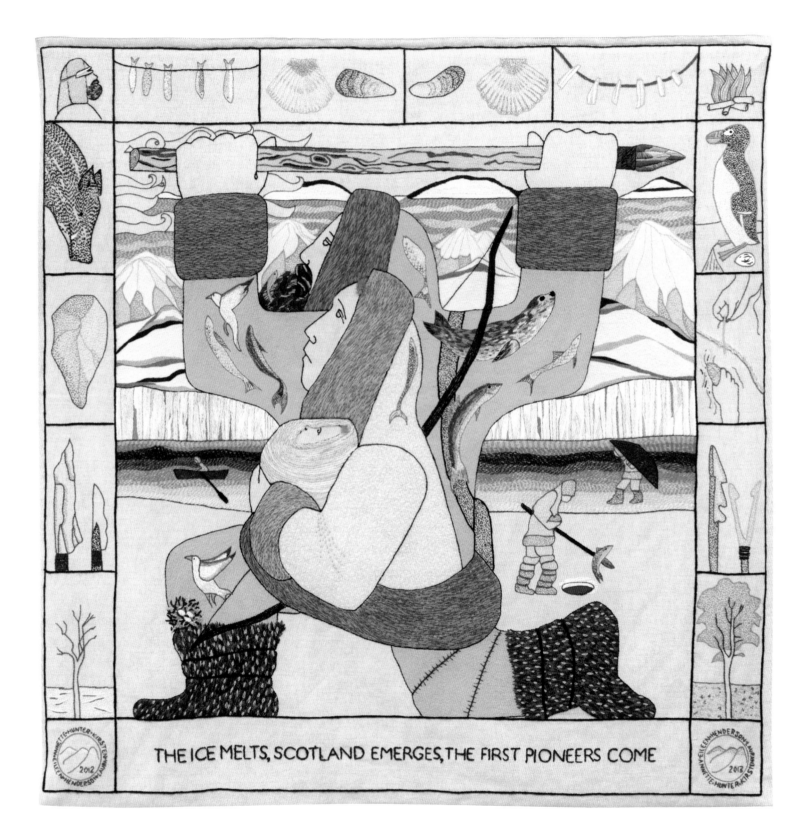

THE ICE MELTS, SCOTLAND EMERGES, THE FIRST PIONEERS COME

PANEL 5 The Wildwood

Panel stitched by:

The Edinburgh Tapestry Tenners

Jo Avery
Joy Dunn
Joan Houston
Joan Leslie
Morag Macleod
Elizabeth McCall Smith
Elizabeth McGuigan
Gill Salvesen
Katherine Shaw
Liz Sutherland
Marjory Watson
Susan Wexler
Nikhat Yusaf

Stitched in:
Linlithgow, Edinburgh

After the ice, willow scrub was the first to colonise, growing in sheltered, damp places, and then came aspen, birch, hazel, elm, oak and finally lime. As they grew and the leaves of a thousand autumns fell and enriched the soil, Scotland was carpeted by a vast wildwood – a green and temperate jungle that stretched away on every horizon. By the end of the eighth millennium BC, deciduous trees could thrive and survive at 2,500 feet above sea level and only in the windblown Highland ranges would the wildwood fail to grow. With the trees and the dense canopy came animals which nested, burrowed and browsed in the shade at ground level, living off a plenitude of insects, seeds, leaves, grasses, roots and shoots. But there was also drama. The aurochs, giant wild cattle with seven-foot hornspreads, thrashed through the undergrowth and wild boar, especially sows with young, could be a fearsome sight on the charge. Red and roe deer and elk also flitted amongst the shadows of the trees. Streams, rivers and lochs were home to fish, waterfowl, otters and beavers while all were closely followed by their predators – wolves, lynxes and bears. And, principal amongst them, the first Pioneers to arrive after the ice. It may well be that the animals of the wildwood saw people so rarely that they were more curious than afraid. They soon learned to be.

THE WILD WOOD AND ITS FAUNA c8500 BC

PANEL 6 Tents and Tipis

Panel stitched by:

Halflinbarns Schoolhouse Weaving Group

Vi Bathgate
Frances Fergusson
Frances Gardiner
Beth Orr
Irene Rendells
Diane Rendells
Muriel Stuart

Stitched in:
North Berwick, East Linton

The Pioneers at first left only gossamer traces. At Cramond, near Edinburgh, the postholes left by the whippy green rods needed to make a bender tent encampment have been found and dated to the ninth millennium BC. And more spectacular, larger postholes were excavated at Barns Ness in East Lothian and interpreted as the earliest substantial house yet found in Scotland. This remarkable find closely resembled a similar structure unearthed at Howick, in Northumberland, and, in 2013, another was found at Echline during the construction of the Queensferry Crossing, on the south side of the Forth. Each had been made from whole tree trunks rammed into postholes and canted inwards to form a tipi shape. This frame was then covered by turf or perhaps thatch made with bracken and ferns. The living space was an oval shape and could accommodate a family of seven or eight. But the importance of these ancient houses was that they signified ownership of the land around them or at least the exercise of customary rights. Why expend all that energy if others could fish and hunt nearby? The most important resource was firewood for heat, cooking and light and many bands of hunter-gatherers will have ranged wide to gather it and possibly been forced to move when wood became scarce. Very few people lived in Scotland at the time the houses at Barns Ness and Echline were built – perhaps no more than a thousand or so. If these houses were occupied at the same time, the family bands who lived in them may have known each other.

TUNDRA SEAL SKIN MESOLITHIC CANOE PADDLES BASS ROCK HUNTERS

VENISON DOGGERLAND

FISHING GATHERERS

HAZELNUT COOKING

DOG WHELK-SALT DYE FLINTS

ENCAMPMENT AT CRAMOND
SCOTLAND'S FIRST HOUSE AT BARN'S NESS, EAST LOTHIAN c8,000 BC

PANEL 7 The First Farmers

Panel stitched by:

Jo Constantine
Rebecca Fish
Frances Gardiner
Moira Gunn
Rosalind Neville-Smith
Hazel Shearer
Molly Shearer
Dorie Wilkie

Stitched in:
Orkney, North Berwick

In the years around c. 3,000 BC, the greatest revolution in Scotland's history took place. Farmers crossed the North Sea from Europe and they brought new techniques of cultivating crops and domesticating animals. Life changed utterly and amongst many spectacular monuments to the productivity of the farmers were the great stone circles of Orkney and the large timber halls built on the banks of rivers in eastern Scotland at places such as Balbridie, Claish and Kelso. The population grew very quickly particularly as a consequence of growing cereal crops. It turns out that the invention of porridge changed the world. In hunter-gatherer societies infants with soft baby teeth found the wild harvest of roots, fruits, nuts and berries difficult and consequently they were breastfed for much longer. While nursing, women generally cannot conceive and so the birth interval was long. When cereal cultivation began, the dried or charred grains could be mashed into a protein-rich porridge and fed to infants. This allowed mothers to stop breast-feeding earlier and it greatly reduced the birth interval so the first farmers began to have much larger families. And the production of food surpluses in good years allowed these growing communities the time to do work not associated with agriculture – the building of the great religious monuments of prehistoric Scotland.

LIMPET · SHETLAND SHEEP · PIEROWALL STONE · UNSTAN WARE · WHELK

WESTRAY WIFEY

PINS

GROOVED WARE

WHEAT

MAES HOWE

SKARA BRAE

RING OF BRODGAR

THE GREAT HALL of BALBRIDIE

BRODGAR BOY

BULL'S HORN

TOOLS

BARLEY

WESTRAY

THE FIRST FARMERS BUILD THEIR MONUMENTS c3,000 BC

PANEL 8 Brochs, Crannogs and Cairns

Panel stitched by:

Dianne Laing
Frances Gardiner

Stitched in:
North Berwick

With no windows, only one door and a double skin of thick drystane walls, the remarkable structures known as brochs may seem like a response to Scotland's weather. Most were built towards the end of the first millennium BC in the Northern Isles and around the Atlantic coasts although isolated examples were found near Galashiels and in Berwick-shire. Brochs were almost certainly status symbols probably built by specialist teams of masons for important individuals. They stand as what archaeologists call 'statements in the landscape'. No doubt warm and relatively spacious with two or three floors, they were not easily defended. Crannogs were. Raised on wooden piles driven into the beds of lochs, just offshore, these houses were surrounded by water and accessible only by a single wooden causeway. Loch Tay had several along its banks. Crannogs were a watery variant on the roundhouse, a design that evolved in later prehistory in Scotland. Conical in shape, the roof beams usually rested on a low circular stone wall and the house was made weather tight by turf or bracken thatch. Some were large with diameters of 33 to 36 feet and had two storeys. Cairns were more enigmatic. Often found on hilltops, they may have been memorials or places where the worship of sky gods took place. Such beliefs may have been more common amongst the Carnonacae of Wester Ross and the coastal glens down to Skye. Their presence was noted on a map made in the second century AD and their name means the People of the Cairns.

PANEL 9 Pytheas the Greek

Panel stitched by:

Margaret Macleod
Mary Macleod

Stitched in:
Isle of Lewis

The first traveller to leave any sort of a record of his journey to Scotland was Pytheas, a Greek traveller and explorer from the mercantile colony of Massalia, modern Marseilles. Some time around 320 BC, he came north to visit Britain, possibly because the tin miners of Cornwall exported the metal to the Mediterranean for the production of the alloy known as bronze. Or perhaps he was just curious. In any case, Pytheas gave our country its name. He called it Pretannike, the land of the Pretannikoi, the People of the Tattoos. Probably conferred by the kindreds who lived on the southern coasts of the Channel, it referred to the habit of body decoration, something that had probably died out on the Continent and made the peoples of Britain different. Almost certainly transported in curraghs, sea-going hide boats sailed by experienced local merchants and mariners, Pytheas circumnavigated Britain. Using a measuring stick called a gnomon, he took a reading of latitude on the Isle of Lewis, probably at the ancient stone circle at Calanais. Intrepid and inquisitive, the Greek explorer travelled further north to Orkney and Shetland and perhaps even beyond. The record of his journey, *On the Ocean*, has been lost but it was so widely referred to – and mocked – by other writers in antiquity that large parts of it can be reconstructed. When the Romans came to conquer, almost four centuries later, they altered Pretannike to Britannia. If they had not, we might all be called the Prits rather than the Brits.

58° N

MUIR IS TIR

Isle of Lewis Stitchers

PYTHEAS CIRCUMNAVIGATES SCOTLAND c320 BC VISITS CALANAIS

PANEL 10 The Coming of the Legions

Panel stitched by:

Caroline M Buchanan
Anne Hamill
Susan Lindsay

Stitched in:
Larbert, Falkirk

In AD 43, the Emperor Claudius entered Colchester in triumph at the head of his victorious legions, their eagle standards glinting, hob-nailed boots tramping. To impress the defeated British kindreds, they had even brought war elephants to plod past the crowds. In the following forty years, the Romans pushed the edges of their Empire farther and farther northwards until the governor of the province of Britannia, Julius Agricola, led an invasion force into Scotland. Having brigaded together three legions and regiments of auxiliaries, he marched his men up through the Tayside and Angus glens to a place the Romans called the Graupian Mountain. Probably at the foot of Bennachie in Aberdeenshire, a pivotal battle was fought. A confederacy of Caledonian kindreds commanded by Calgacus, the first Scot to be named in the historical record, was defeated by the discipline, determination and organisation of the legions and auxiliaries. But the victory was not consolidated, Scotland was soon abandoned and Agricola recalled to Rome. Some time around 122, the Emperor Hadrian ordained that a wall should be built. It stretched from near the mouth of the Tyne, through the Hexham Gap to the Solway coast beyond Carlisle. It was as much a clear limit to conquest as a means of controlling the frontier between the province of Britannia and the barbarians of the north, an early definition of Scotland. The south of Scotland was briefly part of the Empire in the middle of the second century when Hadrian's successor, Antoninus Pius, commanded a turf wall to be raised between the Forth and Clyde. But it was a short-lived occupation. Several Roman commentators grumbled that Scotland was simply not worth the bother.

MONS GRAUPIUS 83 AD THE ROMANS BUILD WALLS

PANEL 11   Ninian at Whithorn

Panel stitched by:

Shirley McKeand

Stitched in:
Dumfries

Carlisle appears to have survived as a functioning Roman town for at least two centuries after the fall of the Western Roman Empire. When St Cuthbert visited in 685, he was shown a working fountain, something that implied a working water supply. Early Christianity in Britain flourished principally amongst town dwellers and there seems to have been a well-established church in the town served by ordained priests. Carlisle may have been the place where Ninian himself was instructed and ordained. His dates are a matter for constant revision but he probably preached some time in the fifth century. At the ancient church of Whithorn in Galloway, what is known as the Latinus Stone was found. It seems not to have been a tombstone but rather the commemoration of the foundation of a shrine or a monastic refuge of some kind. Perhaps it remembers the mission of Ninian who, according to a slightly confused account from Bede of Jarrow written in the early eighth century, had been sent to convert 'the Southern Picts'. This last is probably a vague reference, from a monk who never left the twin monasteries of Monkwearmouth and Jarrow, to the native kindreds of the Novantae and the Selgovae, the early peoples of Galloway and Dumfries. Ninian caused a church to be built at Whithorn and it was notable because it was made in stone 'which was unusual amongst the British' sniffed the sainted Bede. It was known as Candida Casa, the White House, and the aura of sanctity around Ninian's foundation has endured for more than 1,500 years.

CANDIDA CASA

ROME

DINAN · RINGAN

RYNGEN

NINIAS · NYNIA · NINUS

RICNA

TRYNNIAN · NINNIDH

NINIAN AT WHITHORN c400 AD

PANEL 12 Dalriada

Panel stitched by:

Felicity Blackburn
Catherine Borthwick
Helen Brodie
Morag Keenan
Eileen MacPhie
Linda McLean
Heather Simpson

Stitched in:
Arisaig, Malliag, Edinburgh

In the fifth century AD and perhaps for some time before, Irish war bands had been crossing the North Channel to invade and to settle. DNA evidence supports the notion of colonisation by Northern Irish kindreds, in particular those known as the Ui Neill. They seized the Atlantic coastlines of Argyll (the name means the Coast of the Gael), several southern Hebridean islands and the shores of Lorne and further north. In their mouths, these warriors and settlers brought the Gaelic language to replace the Pictish dialects of those they subdued. For many centuries afterwards, Gaelic was described as Irish or Erse. Dalriada became the collective name, according to Bede, for the territory of the incomers and eventually its kings became powerful right across Scotland. Recent research has discovered a frontier between the British kingdom of Strathclyde and the Dalriadan Gaels. It is marked by the Clach nam Breatainn, the Stone of the Britons, at the head of Loch Lomond in the north and in the south in the Firth of Clyde by the sentinel Cumbraes, literally the islands of the British. One of the earliest Scottish historical documents to survive is the *Senchus Fer n-Alban*, the *History of the Men of Alba*, now the Gaelic name for all Scotland but then a reference only to Dalriada. It is a naval muster roll and it describes a seaborne warrior culture, something that would endure for a millennium or more. More peacefully, the Irish invaders eventually brought Columba to Scotland and to Iona, surely the spiritual heart of the West.

NIALL NOIGIALLACH

IRISH WARBANDS INVADE
DALRIADA FOUNDED. COLUMBA AT IONA 563 AD. DUNADD

PANEL 13 Cuthbert and the Gospels

Panel stitched by:

Stitchers o' Stow

Anna Houston
Helen Houston
Lorna Lyons
Patricia McMahon
Diana Muir
Karen Nelson
Serpil Renton
Amanda Runciman
Kathleen Runciman
Libby Runciman
Elizabeth Simm
Dorothy Small
Deborah Wood

with stitches from the children
of Stow Primary School

Stitched in:
Stow, Galashiels, Lauder

Some time in the late seventh century, a young man rode from the hills above Melrose to the gate of the old Celtic monastery that lay in a loop of the River Tweed. Cuthbert wished to become a monk and lead an exemplary life of prayer, contemplation and preaching. He became Bishop of Lindisfarne and, shortly after his death on the tidal island, he was canonised. And immediately claimed by the English. The reality is more complicated. Cuthbert is an Anglian name but, in the seventh century, the Borders and the Lothians formed part of the glittering kingdom of Northumbria and would remain so for more than three centuries. A northern dialect of early English would develop into Scots and it was introduced by the Angles of the Tweed Basin and the Lothians. Surely the most beautiful and dramatic in Britain, Durham Cathedral was raised on Cuthbert's bones and his saintly cult brought pilgrims, gifts and money to his tomb and those who tended it. His name supplied an early definition of Englishness when the people who lived to the south of the Tweed began to call themselves the Haliwerfolc, the People of the Holy Man. But, in truth, these claims and counterclaims pale into insignificance beside the glorious achievements of the church in the north between the seventh and ninth centuries. The Book of Kells was essentially a production of the Columban monastery at Iona and the Lindisfarne Gospels were made by the island monks in their windblown refuge off the Northumberland coast. Perhaps one day these stunning artistic and spiritual achievements will come back home where they belong.

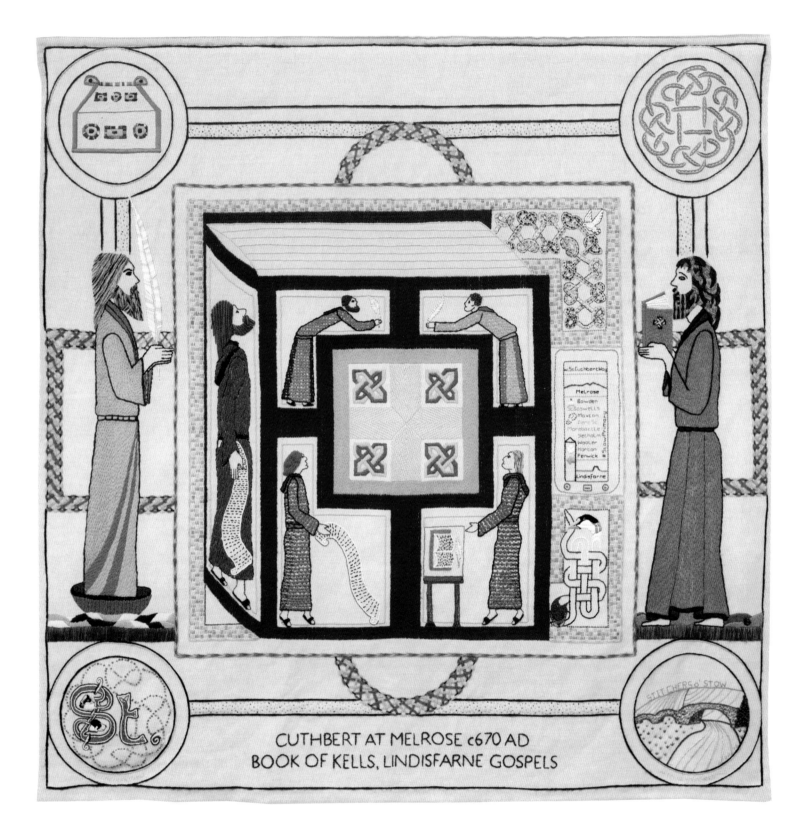

CUTHBERT AT MELROSE c670 AD
BOOK OF KELLS, LINDISFARNE GOSPELS

PANEL 14 The Crosses and the Angles

Panel stitched by:

The Angle Stitchers

Helen Allan
Margaret Boe
Georgina Chapman
Barbara Downie
Amelia Little
Yvonne Tweedie
Frea Webster

Stitched in:
Edinburgh, Haddington

When the ambitious and ruthless kings of Northumbria pushed west with their war bands in the late seventh and eighth centuries, they obliterated the ancient British kingdom of Rheged. Hinged on Carlisle, it stretched as far west as Dunragit, or the Fort of Rheged, near Stranraer, and perhaps as far south as Lancashire. In the wake of the warriors came holy men and artists. Two of the most beautiful and intricate examples of early Christian sculpture in Britain stand at Bewcastle, on the moors east of Carlisle, and at Ruthwell, in Dumfriesshire. Scenes from scripture were carved on the cross shafts and arms and brightly painted. The Ruthwell Cross also has a place in the story of British literature. Carved in Northumbrian runes cut on the lower, narrow sides of the shaft are two extracts from one of the earliest surviving poems composed in English, *The Dream of the Rood*. It is part of a very sophisticated scheme of words and images for reading the cross and its central conceit is that the rood or cross upon which Christ was crucified had a personality. This is the haunting second stanza:

> I [lifted up] a powerful king –
> The Lord of Heaven I dared not tilt.
> Men insulted both of us together;
> I was drenched with blood poured from the man's side.

RUTHWELL AND BEWCASTLE CROSSES
AND THE ARRIVAL OF THE ANGLES, 7th TO 9th CENTURY

PANEL 15 Dunnichen

Panel stitched by:

*Angus Embroidery and
Textile Artists*

Pat Beaton
Norman Beaton
Dot Chalmers
Linda Clark
Betty Fotheringham
Elspeth Foxworthy
Helen Fulford
Elizabeth Hill
Isobel Hyslop
Deborah Kenward
Janette Nairn
Ena Norrie
Patricia Rae
Joan Robb
Iolanta Robertson
Mary Stephen
Sandra Taylor
Linda Walker
Margaret Wynne

Stitched in:
Carnoustie, Forfar, Arbroath

Few battles genuinely alter the course of history and even fewer in the early history of Scotland were commemorated by an artist. In the kirkyard at Aberlemno in Angus, there stands a remarkable Pictish stone. Carved on one side are four scenes from the Battle of Dunnichen, fought in 685 only six or so miles from Aberlemno. The sculptor shows a genuine understanding of warfare. There is a shield wall of infantry with the man in the front rank waiting for the shock of a cavalry charge and he holds up a shield with a prominent boss at an angle that might meet a downward cut from a cavalry warrior. Behind him is a soldier holding a long spear that projects well beyond his comrade and behind him stands a third rank ready to support and plug gaps in the line. Warriors on horseback may represent the two great kings whose armies clashed at Dunnichen. The Picts were led by Bridei and the Angles by Ecgfrith. Having conquered the Tweed Valley, the Lothians and probably Fife, the Anglian juggernaut had rumbled northwards to be met by Bridei and his war bands at Dunnichen, near Forfar, where it was brought to a juddering halt. Ecgfrith was killed and the Angles retreated south of the Forth. Bridei's achievement was not only a decisive victory; it made Scotland possible. If the Northumbrians had won and gained control of fertile Pictland, consolidating as they did in the south, England and the English language might have stretched all the way to Shetland.

THE PICTS DEFEAT THE ANGLES AT DUNNICHEN 685 AD

PANEL 16 The Vikings

Panel stitched by:

Gaels Stitchers

Sheila Forrest
Heather Forrest
Catherine Harrison
Madalene Lee
Ann MacGilp
Maureen McKellar
Maureen Robinson
Margaret Smith
Mary Swift

Stitched in:
Dunoon

In 793, fell portents were seen. Thunder and lightning rent the air and dragons flew. On the shingle beach of the holy island of Lindisfarne, fearsome warriors rasped their ships up above the high-tide line and raced for the doors of the monastery before the terrified monks could bolt them. The Vikings had sailed into history. Even across thirteen centuries the shock of the first attacks is still palpable. The outrage of the church was expressed in an early description: the Vikings were known as the Sons of Death. Their *dreki* or dragon ships were sleek, fast and very versatile, able to deliver warriors to targets that lay inland but up navigable rivers, their shallow draught taking the keels clear of reefs of sand or rocks and their double-ended hulls allowing them to reverse in narrow channels. After the first raids, Vikings began to colonise parts of Scotland. Orkney and Shetland retain the clearest Scandinavian cultural and genetic legacies while almost all the place names on the Isle of Lewis are Norse in origin. Some names recall how the Viking sea lords saw Scotland as a landmass articulated by a series of sea roads. The place name Tarbert – there is a Tarbert in Kintyre and another between Loch Lomond and Loch Long (and the Firth of Clyde) – means 'an overbring-ing', a place where crews trundled their longships overland, probably by pulling them on log rollers.

VIKINGS DRAG LONGSHIP OVER THE ISTHMUS AT TARBERT, ARGYLL

DUNOON

ARGYLL

THE COMING OF THE VIKINGS

PANEL 17 Dumbarton Rock

Panel stitched by:

Artgal's Rocks

Maud Crawford
Louise Foster
Ashley Holdsworth
Linda Jobson
Patricia Livingston
Sarah Muir
Mary Richardson
Julie Robertson
Dorie Wilkie

Stitched in:
Glasgow, Edinburgh

In the summer of 870, lookouts on the ancient fortress of Dumbarton Rock saw a bone-chilling sight. Rounding the headland and gliding into the upper Clyde were the sails of more than two hundred Viking dragon ships. Standing in the prows of the most splendid were sea lords and the Norse kings of York and Dublin. They had come to lay siege to the Rock of the Clyde, Alcluith, the seat of the Old-Welsh-speaking kings of Strathclyde, Ystrad Clud. After four months of bitter attrition, the well on the Rock ran dry and the garrison was forced to surrender. Instead of slaughter, the Strathclyde aristocracy faced slavery. The Vikings carried on a widespread and lucrative trade and elite captives will have fetched high prices at the slave market in Dublin. King Artgal appears to have evaded capture but he had the greater misfortune to fall into the hands of King Constantine of Alba or Scotland, the son of Kenneth MacAlpin. The last independent king of Strathclyde was executed. The siege and the failure of its dynasty appeared to spell the end of the ancient kingdom as a separate polity but its name and crown lingered in the records for more than a century after Artgal's death. At the Battle of Carham in 1018, there was a final flourish. King Owain of Strathclyde rode south with his war band to join the forces of Malcolm II of Scotland in an attack on the Angles of Northumbria. But, by the middle of the 11th century, no more is heard of the rulers who held court on the spectacular Rock of the Clyde.

THE VIKINGS TAKE DUMBARTON ROCK 870 AD

PANEL 18 Constantine Climbs the Hill of Faith

Panel stitched by:

Constant Stitchers

Katie Antonio
Helen Huxley
Dorothy Maingot

Stitched in:
Perth, Glencarse

The unrelenting pressure exerted by Viking sea lords in the Hebrides and along the Atlantic shore helped push the focus of an emerging Scottish kingship eastwards. Scone became important and, when Constantine succeeded to the throne, he and his Bishop of St Andrews, Cellach, made an important public declaration:

> [They] pledged themselves upon the Hill of Faith near the royal city of Scone, that the laws and disciplines of the Faith, and the rights in churches and gospels, should be kept in conformity with [the customs of] the Scots.

Constantine may have been the first to call himself King of Alba, still the Gaelic name for Scotland. This choice and the clear will to mould a national church after a Scottish/Gaelic model can be seen as an explicit rejection of Pictishness – Alba not Pictavia – but it can also be interpreted as a declaration of unity, a conscious and public attempt to weld together disparate parts into a new kingdom. In the 10th century, Scotland spoke the dialects of at least six languages – Norse, Gaelic, Pictish, Old Welsh, Scots and, for the cultured, Latin. The name of Scotia for the lands north of the Forth was current in the 11th century but it was not until the late Middle Ages that Scotland began to be widely used for the whole nation. But it may be said that the idea of Scotland was much in Constantine's mind as he and Cellach climbed the Hill of Faith at Scone.

CINAED MAC AILPIN

DUNNOTTAR

AED MAC CINAEDA

ALBA

CONSTANTINE CLIMBS THE HILL OF FAITH 904 AD

GLENCARSE
DM
PITCAIRNGREEN
HH
ST KA
MARTINS

PANEL 19 Carham

Panel stitched by:

Jane Cole
Val Fairbairn
Mig Moore
Carolyn Scott
Isa Scott
Margaret Waller
Moira Wilson

Stitched in:
Tweedbank, Galashiels

In the summer of 1018, on the banks of the River Tweed, Scottish axemen swung their weapons to brutal effect as they cut a Northumbrian war band to pieces. Led by Malcolm II and King Owain of Strathclyde, the Scots broke the ranks of the Northumbrian spearmen of Uhtred, Earl of Northumbria. Carham is now a tiny, sleepy hamlet on the English bank of the river but, to the emerging Scottish kings, it was a place of great significance. The Tweed Valley had been part of the kingdom and earldom for three centuries, it spoke English and shared a common culture, from matters of religion to agriculture. But Malcolm's axemen chopped through these ancient ties to make an emphatic statement – that the Tweed Valley was now part of the kingdom of Scotland. English chroniclers attached much less importance to the battle. Some indeed believed that this fertile swathe of territory had been granted to Kenneth II of Scotland by the English King Edgar in 981. But Malcolm II may not only have been fighting a force mustered from the lands south of the Tweed, he may also have been asserting himself over people to the north who still saw themselves as Anglian. It took more than a century before the Tweed Basin thought of itself as not English and it may be that Carham was the bloody beginning of a transition.

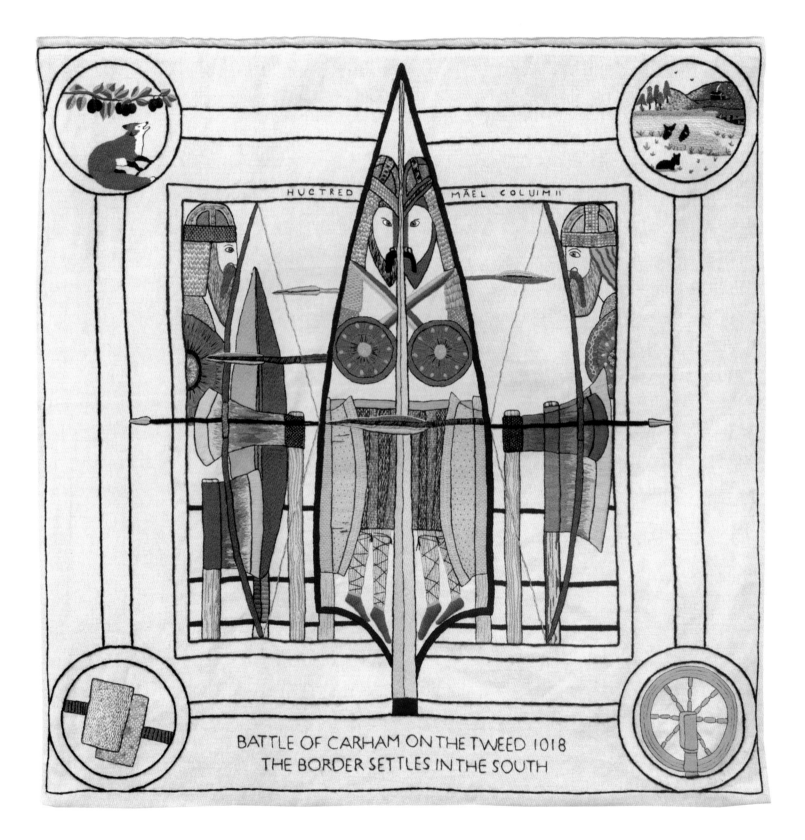

HUCTRED   MÄEL COLUIM II

BATTLE OF CARHAM ON THE TWEED 1018
THE BORDER SETTLES IN THE SOUTH

PANEL 20 King Macbeth

Panel stitched by:

Sandra Leith
Glennie Leith
Ingrid McGown
Paddy McGruer
Rhea Scott

Stitched in:
Moray, Portsoy

The famous play by William Shakespeare may be seen as five acts of unrelenting defamation. Guilty of none of the foul crimes enacted on stages all over the world, Macbeth was, in reality, a competent monarch whose kingdom was sufficiently peaceful for him to go on pilgrimage to Rome. There, he was said to have scattered money like seed and no doubt sought papal forgiveness for only the most routine of sins. Almost never given his royal rank, Macbeth was a king twice over. From the early 1030s, he was King of Moray, an ancient polity around the shores of the Moray Firth, and, when King Duncan of Alba invaded in 1040, he was killed – in battle not in bed. Aside from resistance from Crinan (lay abbot of Dunkeld), the Abbot of Iona and young (not old) Duncan's father, King Macbeth of Alba ruled unchallenged and legitimately for 14 years. In 1054, Siward, Earl of Northumbria, raided deep into Scotland and began a process of destabilisation which ended in King Macbeth's death in 1057. He was succeeded by his stepson, Lulach. Almost erased from the regnal lists, King Lulach reigned for only a year before being deposed by Malcolm III. Far from being the ruthless, wicked, witch-obsessed tyrant of the Scottish play, King Macbeth was lauded as 'the renowned' after his death and, in *The Prophecy of Berchan*, the author sang of 'the generous king' and 'the red, tall, golden-haired one, he will be pleasant to me among them; Scotland will be brimful west and east during the reign of the furious red one'. King Macbeth was famous as *Ri Deircc*, 'the Red King'. Perhaps his red hair was traduced into red blood. Whaur's yer Willie Shakespeare noo?

BOW FIDDLE ROCK

THREE KINGS

BATTLE OF THE BAUDS

THE BOOK OF DEER

FORDYCE
STRIVE TO ACHIEVE

KING MACBETH IN MORAY 1050s

PANEL 21 St Margaret of Scotland

Panel stitched by:

St Margaret's Stitchers

Brenda Borrows
Rebecca Brown
Vonny Burke
Beryl Butcher
Sally Clark
Agnes Mabon
Kate McDonald

Stitched in:
Dalgety Bay, Aberdour,
Dunfermline, Cairneyhill

Born in Hungary, a princess of the English royal house of Wessex, Margaret fled to Scotland in 1066 after the Norman Conquest. Four year later, she married Malcolm III Canmore (not because of his head, big or otherwise; the nickname was, in fact, a title for, in Gaelic, *Ceann Mhor* means something like 'Great Leader/Ruler'). She was a paragon of piety and fertility. Canonised in 1250, she deserved more immediate recognition for mothering no fewer than five sons and two daughters, all of whom lived to adulthood. This ensured that the MacMalcolm dynasty would not lack heirs. Three of Margaret's sons reigned as kings of Scotland – Edgar, Alexander and David – but it is perhaps for her faith that St Margaret will be remembered. Pilgrimage was becoming increasingly popular in 11th-century Scotland and the queen laid plans to make it easier to visit the great shrine of St Andrew. A ferry for pilgrims ran from South Queensferry to North Queensferry, where the road and rail bridges now stand, and, at North Berwick, a longer crossing could be made to Earlsferry in the East Neuk. In addition, Queen Margaret also worked to bring the Scottish church closer to the papacy in Rome but also did not ignore the sacred sites of the Celtic church when she ensured that Iona's monastery was restored. Many churches (and an excellent university in Edinburgh) are dedicated to her, the oldest being St Margaret's Chapel in Edinburgh Castle, the most venerable building in the city. It was endowed and founded by her equally pious son, David I. Margaret's other signal achievement was to have been one of the few women to take a leading role in our early history.

ST MARGARET AT DUNFERMLINE c1080

PANEL 22 The Flowers of the Borders

Panel stitched by:

*Scottish Borders
Embroiderers' Guild*

Alison Delaney
Catherine Edmondson
Barbara Farquhar
Susan Gray
Ali Halley
Cathy McCulloch
Jenni Young

Stitched in:
Galashiels, Hawick,
St Boswells, Jedburgh,
Melrose

The immense power of religious belief is sometimes underestimated in modern, secular Scotland. The landscape of the 12th-century Border country was punctuated by its products. Eight hundred years ago, it would have looked entirely natural to our eyes. Almost all buildings were made from wood and roofed with bracken or turf. Only the smoke of cooking fires would have drawn our attention. The tallest landmarks on the horizon were trees, roads were no more than narrow tracks and the only substantial man-made structures were the stockaded motte and bailey fortresses being thrown up by local lords – and they were few. But, in four places in the Borders, within a radius of little more than ten miles, piety raised up four mighty churches. Awe-inspiring and vast, the abbeys at Kelso, Jedburgh, Melrose and Dryburgh were a stunning architectural response to a profound depth of belief. Inspired by David I and all founded in the first half of the 12th century, communities of reformed monks came to the south of Scotland to build churches and monasteries. The first and perhaps the most significant were the Tironensians from Picardy in France. After a false start near Selkirk, they moved to a bend in the River Tweed at Kelso. There the construction of a vast cathedral-scale church began. With a double crossing and a collection of conventual buildings around it, Kelso Abbey was a wonder of the age. Now, only part of the west end still stands but it is a truly monumental fragment. At Jedburgh, most of the nave survives and Melrose has a roof as it carried on being used as a parish church. But perhaps the prettiest and most atmospheric of all is Dryburgh, the last resting place of Sir Walter Scott and Earl Haig. The abbeys were lavishly patronised and sometimes wealthy and anxious noblemen who knew they were dying gave gifts that involved them becoming novice monks, thus qualifying for burial inside the sacred precincts. This taking of holy orders was *ad succurrundum*, done in a hurry. They believed that the soil of the precinct would cleanse their bodies of sin.

MELROSE · DRYBURGH · KELSO · JEDBURGH ·

THE GREAT BORDER ABBEYS ARE BUILT

PANEL 23 David I and the Wool Trade

Panel stitched by:

*Broomlands/
Roxburghshire WRI*

Kathleen Binnie
Elizabeth Bruce
Val Horsburgh
Cathy Simpson
Joan Turnbull
Val Van Der Reijden
Hazel Woodsell

Stitched in:
Kelso

Prosperity as well as piety raised the Border abbeys, St Andrews and Glasgow Cathedrals and the other great churches of early medieval Scotland. Much wealth was accumulated by the rapid development of the wool trade. As well-organised and semi-industrial textile production intensified in Flanders and Italy, the demand for raw wool grew. And, in the relatively benign climate of the 12th century, the monasteries in the Borders ran huge sheep ranches in the Cheviots (and there were others in the likes of the Lammermuirs – the Lambs' Moors) and a busy inland market was established at the royal burgh of Roxburgh. This enormously important medieval town has been entirely effaced; not one stone has been left standing upon another, a casualty of centuries of border warfare with England. But it saw the beginning of urban life in Scotland. Once the spring clip had taken place and the fleeces had been baled into woolpacks, sold at Roxburgh and either carted or possibly floated on rafts down the Tweed to Berwick, they were loaded at the quays on to ships bound for the Low Countries and further afield. Berwick became a very wealthy town, the location of groups of foreign merchants and the largest contributor of customs revenues to the crown. David I and his successors created royal burghs to stimulate trade and bring Scotland into the mainstream of the European economy. Until the Wars of Independence destroyed Roxburgh and ultimately severed the arterial link with Berwick, Scotland prospered on the backs of its sheep.

BURGHS

ELGIN · ABERDEEN · MONTROSE · PERTH · ST ANDREWS · STIRLING · DUNFERMLINE · LINLITHGOW · EDINBURGH · PEEBLES

RUTHERGLEN · LANARK

SAIR SANCT FOR THE CROON

CANONGATE · HADDINGTON

BERWICK · ROXBURGH

CHANGED THE COARSE STUFFS OF HIS OWN LAND FOR PRICELESS VESTMENTS AND COVERED ITS ANCIENT NAKEDNESS WITH PURPLE AND LINEN

RENFREW · FORRES

S·W·R·I

ROXBURGHSHIRE FEDERATION

HGW   VMH   LT   CMS

KSB

KELSO ABBEY 2013

EMB   V∞R

DAVID I FOSTERS THE WOOL TRADE c1130s

PANEL 24 St Andrews Cathedral

Panel stitched by:

*Hill of Tarvit Textile
Conservation Volunteers NTS*

Christeen Anderson
Soan Cairns
Alison Docherty
Ursula Doherty
Anne Halford McLeod
Margaret May
Ann Miller

Stitched in:
Cupar, Auchtermuchty,
Dairsie, Upper Largo,
Newport on Tay, Ceres

Only two shrines in Western Europe housed the relics of the Apostles, men who had known Jesus. One was St James at Santiago de Compostela in Northern Spain and the other was St Andrew at St Andrews. According to legend, St Regulus, a Greek monk from Patras, brought three finger bones of the saint's right hand, the upper bone of an arm, a kneecap and a tooth. By 1070, these had been housed in St Regulus' Church, now in the precincts of St Andrews Cathedral, its 33-metre-high tower a famous landmark. By the 13th century, and probably earlier, St Andrew was seen as the patron saint of Scotland and the possession of his relics was a powerful buttress for the emergence of a national church. He had been crucified on the crux decussata, the diagonals of the St Andrews Cross, the saltire flag of Scotland. In the middle of the prosperous 12th century, the construction of a grand cathedral to hold the relics was begun and it continued for more than a century. It was finally dedicated in 1318 in the presence of King Robert the Bruce. The town plan of St Andrews reflected the cathedral's central importance with North and South Streets laid out as processional ways leading to and from the West Door. By the time of the Scottish Reformation in the middle of the 16th century, the great church was stripped of its altars and images and the relics of St Andrew lost. Stone robbers removed much of the fabric and now the east gable stands almost alone as the most impressive reminder of the cathedral's medieval grandeur.

VIDERUNT

OMNES FINES

TERRAE SALUTARE

DEI NOSTRI

ST ANDREWS CATHEDRAL

NTS
HILL OF TARVIT

PANEL 25 Duns Scotus and the Schoolmen

Panel stitched by:

*Embroiderers' Guild
Kelso Branch*

Ann Bacon
Mary Bonsor
Elizabeth Cuthbert
Stephanie Dempsey
Kay Gardiner
Colina Harris-Burland
Tricia Marshall
Alison Minter
Margaret Mitchell
Pat Nicol
Tricia Reynolds
Anita Rhind
Rineke Sangster
Anne White
Helen Williams

Stitched in:
Coldstream, Tweedmouth,
Hawick, Ednam, Gordon,
Kelso, Duns

The local and correct pronunciation of the Berwickshire town of Duns is 'dunce' and the name may not be mocked for it arose in its other usage from the philosophy of one of the greatest intellectuals of the Middle Ages. Probably born in or near the town c. 1266, John Duns (or Dunce) Scotus was ordained in the priesthood in the Order of the Friars Minor in Northampton. They were popularly known as the Franciscans. Towards the end of 1302, John began teaching at the University of Paris. In his copious and hugely influential writings, he produced elegant arguments for the existence of God, the reality of the Immaculate Conception and much else. Scotus's work was widely admired and his followers were sometimes known as Schoolmen or Scholastics. His work remains important and, in the 20th century, there was a significant resurgence of interest and admiration. Philosophers such as Peter King, Gyula Klima, Paul Vincent Spade and others acknowledged his immense contribution to western thought. But, in the 16th century, John Duns Scotus's reputation was much dented. When his supporters opposed the work of Renaissance humanists and their fascination with classical – and pagan – philosophers such as Aristotle and Plato, and in particular the creation of the King James Bible, they were derided as Dunsmen or Dunces – people incapable of good scholarship. But modern dunces should be much consoled by their close association with one of Scotland's greatest minds and one of our most beautiful counties.

DUNS SCOTUS AND THE SCHOOLMEN

PANEL 26 Somerled, Lord of the Isles

Panel stitched by:

Becky Dacre
Jill Gosney
Katherine Maclean
Seonaid Macleod
Maria Townsend

Stitched in:
Lochaber

Technological change often drives politics in unexpected directions. The Hebridean warship known as the birlinn developed from the Viking *dreki*, the 'dragon ships'. *Naibhig* in Gaelic, meaning 'the little ships', they were smaller than the longships and much more manoeuvrable as a result not only of scale but a simple innovation. The pilots of the *dreki* used a steer board (the derivation of starboard because the steer board was usually on the right-hand side) attached to the side of the ship but the birlinns were fitted with a hinged rudder fixed to the keel and therefore in the centre. Over the shallow and rocky coastal waters of the Hebrides, these fast and nimble little ships could go places larger boats with a deeper draught dared not. The birlinns were central to the power of Somerled. Sometimes known as Somerled the Viking, his name is from Sumar-lidi or Summer Raider. Rising to prominence through a mixture of conquest and judicious marriage, he established himself as Lord of the Isles, ruling over an Atlantic principality that included many of the islands of the Southern Hebrides and Argyll. In 1156, Somerled and his captains won a great naval battle against Godred Olafsson and by 1158 he had seized Godred's kingdom of Man and the Northern Hebrides. But Somerled's ambitions were not satisfied. In 1164, he sailed a huge army up the Clyde to attack Malcolm IV's kingdom of Scotland. The expedition ended in disaster, Somerled died, the Islesmen retreated and his vast territories broke into smaller lordships. He is seen as the progenitor of Clan Donald and his descendants succeeded to the lordship until the late Middle Ages.

HEBRIDES

KNOYDART

ARDNAMURCHAN

KINTYRE

ISLE OF MAN

RJD SML ATH-THARRACAILL MTT ZKM JEG

SOMERLED, FIRST LORD OF THE ISLES c1160

PANEL 27 Haakon at Kyleakin

Panel stitched by:

South Skye Stitchers

Margaret Scott
Margaret Govier
Laila Hall
Ann Hickey
Julie Mace
Emma Morrison
Flora Struthers

Stitched in:
Isle of Skye

In the summer of 1263, King Haakon of Norway mustered a huge fleet. Alexander II and his son, Alexander III, were actively attempting to incorporate the Atlantic coastlands and islands into their kingdom of Scotland. The gathering of the vast Norwegian fleet after it had crossed the North Sea must have been a memorable sight for it is remembered in a well-known place name. Kyleakin on the Isle of Skye is from the Kyles or Narrows of Haakon, the place where the king's fleet dropped anchor, gathered intelligence and made plans. By October, the fleet had moved south to occupy the Firth of Clyde, using the shelter of the Cumbraes as an anchorage and a source of water and supplies. Negotiations opened but soon failed and, on a stormy night, several Norwegian ships were driven onshore at Largs. A Scottish force arrived and fierce fighting followed on the beach. It was inconclusive but nevertheless the season and the weather were against Haakon, October being late in the year for a large fleet to be at sea, and they set sail for Norway. Three years later, the Treaty of Perth was agreed and the ancient dispute over the sovereignty of the Hebrides, the Atlantic shore and the Isle of Man was settled in Scotland's favour. But Orkney and Shetland were to remain outside the realm of the MacMalcolm kings and their heirs for another two centuries.

NORTHERN ISLES

BISHOP'S PALACE, KIRKWALL

CASTLE MOIL

N ORWAY

KING HAAKON

HAAKON IV HAAKONSSON

2ND OCTOBER 1263

SOUTHERN ISLES

MSS MG JM FGS LEH EM AH

SOUTH SKYE STITCHERS

EILEAN BÀN

HAAKON'S FLEET AT KYLEAKIN, SKYE
AND BATTLE OF LARGS 1263

PANEL 28 The Death of Alexander III

Panel stitched by:

Fab Four Fifers on the Forth

Dorothy Balfour
Jean Boath
Dilys Campbell
Chris Fair

Stitched in:
Cairneyhill, Dalgety Bay,
Aberdour

The night of 19 March 1286 was stormy. Strong winds whipped up the spindrift off the Firth of Forth, rain spattered the royal feasting hall at Edinburgh Castle. But King Alexander III of Scotland was unabashed – he was celebrating his marriage to the beautiful Yolande de Dreux and, perhaps flushed with wine, he was determined to share her bed that very night. The problem was that his new bride was at the royal manor at Kinghorn, across the storm-tossed Forth. Despite entreaties from his anxious courtiers, Alexander called for his horse to be saddled, rode to South Queensferry and crossed safely. Perhaps all would be well. But, somewhere along the cliff path to Kinghorn, the king became detached from his retinue and his horse probably lost its footing in the wind and the dark. The following morning search parties found Alexander III's body on the beach, at the foot of a steep and rocky slope. His neck was broken. Scotland was immediately plunged into a dynastic crisis. All three of the king's children had died and the heir presumptive was Margaret, the Maid of Norway, his granddaughter. She died before she reached Scotland. Alexander's rashness was to cost his realm dear. After the wind and rain of 19 March 1286, much greater storms burst over Scotland as the kingdom without a king began the nightmare of the Wars of Independence.

QUEENSFERRY

PASSAGE

KING'S WOOD

KINGHORN CASTLE

YOLANDE

QUEN ALYSANDYR OURE KING WES DEDE

DEATH OF ALEXANDER III AT KINGHORN, 1286.

PANEL 29 William Wallace and Andrew Moray

Panel stitched by:

Perth Embroiderers' Guild

Lorna Morrison
Gladys Anderson
Dorothy Lewin
Heather Moir
Anthea Pawley
Michelle Peet
Janice Reid
Wendy Rosier
Mary Ross
Pat Scales
Loretta Whitcomb
Jeanette Yates
Margaret Young

Stitched in:
Perth, Blairgowrie, Methven,
Scone

After the death of Alexander III, what became known as 'The Great Cause' developed momentum as several noble families claimed and contended for the vacant throne. In 1293, Edward I of England judged that John Baliol had the strongest claim but he immediately began to manipulate the new king. When Baliol renounced his homage to Edward, the English immediately invaded and forced the King of Scots to abdicate in a humiliating ceremony where the royal arms were ripped off his surcoat. Edward is said to have commented, 'A man does good business when he rids himself of a turd.' In 1296, Andrew Moray led a rebellion in the north and he was soon joined by a force commanded by William Wallace, a minor nobleman from Ayrshire. His name is written as Le Waleis and may have denoted a family who spoke Old Welsh, the ancient tongue of Strathclyde. At Stirling Bridge, the allies scored a stunning victory in 1297. By allowing only part of a much larger English army to cross the narrow bridge before attacking them, they caused chaos. Retreating English soldiers were driven into the ranks of those behind, the bridge broke down and many drowned. After the battle, Wallace and Moray were proclaimed Guardians of Scotland but it seems that Moray died of his wounds soon afterwards. A year later, fortunes reversed as the English triumphed at Falkirk and Wallace spent seven years evading capture. But, in 1305, he was betrayed and taken to London to suffer the appalling agonies of a traitor's death. Having been dragged naked through the streets, he was hanged and, while still alive, emasculated and eviscerated before being beheaded. Knowing what his fate would be, Wallace asserted at his trial that, since he had never been the subject of Edward I, he could be no traitor. It is a stirring story of defiance to the last.

WILLIAM WALLACE AND ANDREW MORAY 1290s

PANEL 30 Bannockburn

Panel stitched by:

Two Toxophilists

Caroline M Buchanan
Margaret Martin

Stitched in:
Falkirk, Stirling

In the Middle Ages and long before, Stirling was the pivot of Scotland. To the west of the great castle rock, treacherous Flanders Moss stretched and it forced those armies that wished to march north to cross the River Forth below the castle walls. In 1314, Stirling was held by an English garrison besieged by the Scots. Edward II mustered a huge army of more than 2,000 armoured knights, the medieval equivalent of modern tanks, and 16,000 infantry and archers. The English king was looking to confront the man who had had himself crowned King of Scots, Robert the Bruce. His army was probably less than half the size of Edward's but he had the immense advantage of choosing the battleground. He would move his army around it brilliantly. And he forced the squadrons of English heavy cavalry to ride over boggy and tussocky ground, probably at the Carse of Balquiderock, about a mile and a half east of the traditional site. Over two days, a remarkable conflict took place. It began with a famous single combat when Sir Henry de Bohun charged with his lance levelled at King Robert – who flicked the reins of his pony to turn him aside at the last moment and with a backhanded cut, felled the English knight in an instant. A roar went up from the Scottish ranks. It was an omen. Formed up in flexible, mobile squares bristling with spears, the Scots attacked the English heavy cavalry as it struggled on the soft terrain. The squadrons broke and the first day ended with momentum swinging to Bruce. Disarray and disagreement in the English ranks allowed the Scottish squares, or schiltrons, to drive deep into the mass of the English army. Archers could not fire for fear of hitting their own men. Buckling under intense pressure, they retreated and were then routed. Edward fled and the slaughter began. It was an unlikely, telling and famous victory.

IT IS IN TRUTH NOT FOR GLORY, NOR RICHES, NOR HONOURS THAT WE ARE FIGHTING, BUT FOR FREEDOM — FOR THAT ALONE, WHICH NO HONEST MAN GIVES UP BUT WITH LIFE ITSELF

DECLARATION OF ARBROATH

1320

ANE PALFREY LITILL AND JOLY

BANNOCKBURN 1314

PANEL 31 The Rain at Carlisle

Panel stitched by:

Galloway Broderers

Anne Ackerley
Lorraine Challis
Helen Keating
Jane McCandlish
Linda Murtough
Marion Owen
Susie Seed
Margaret Surplice
Ruth Williams

with stitches by Children
of Kirkbean Primary School

Stitched in:
Gatehouse-of-Fleet,
Kirkbean, Castle Douglas,
Melrose, Carsphair

Flushed with victory at Bannockburn, King Robert led an invasion of England and, in the spring of 1315, laid siege to the old Roman city of Carlisle and its dour castle. Heroic resistance was directed by Sir Andrew de Harcla, a local lord who was created Earl of Carlisle for his efforts. But the more compelling reason for the city's survival was not dogged defence – it was rain. That spring, unusually heavy and persistent rain fell all over Europe and, around Carlisle's stout walls, Bruce's siege engines became bogged down and were easily toppled in the soaking ground, his army encampment was washed out and little food could be commandeered locally. It was the beginning of the Little Ice Age, a series of periods of bad and cold weather that was to grip Europe for more than five hundred years. The rain not only drove Bruce from Carlisle in 1315, it continued into 1316 and there was widespread famine across Europe. Crops failed, bread was hugely expensive, no winter forage could be cut and herds and flocks had to be slaughtered. By the summer of 1317, the rain had relented but hunger had depleted and weakened the population. In Scotland, between 10 and 25 per cent of the population had died and food production did not return to normal until the mid 1320s. Medieval governments simply could not deal with the crisis caused by climate change and famine and criminal activity became common as people were forced to steal to live. But it was religious faith that may have been rocked most severely. Prayer and intercession had no effect and the 14th century saw the rise of new beliefs across Europe – what were immediately cast as heretical sects.

BRUCE'S SIEGE OF CARLISLE 1315
AND BEGINNING OF LITTLE ICE AGE

PANEL 32   The Black Death

Panel stitched by:

Michael Blacklock
Catherine Hamilton
Liz Sanderson

Stitched in:
Melrose, St Boswells

At Caddonfoot near Galashiels, a Scottish army gathered for a raid into England. Their captains saw what they called 'the foul death of the English' – the devastating arrival of the Black Death in the summer of 1348 – as an opportunity. Believing that this English disease would not affect them, the army attacked Durham and brought the contagion back north. By 1350, it was raging through towns, villages and farm places. Originating in China, the Black Death swept west to Europe and spread quickly to England where it killed between 30 and 50 per cent of the inhabitants – between 3 and 5 million people. Those figures may have been a little less disastrous in Scotland but not by much. The plague was carried by fleas and infected human beings through contact with rats. Also known as bubonic plague, it attacked the lymph glands to cause swelling and then made its deadly way into the bloodstream. A variant was pneumonic plague and it was transmitted through the air rather than by touch. Death was rapid – only three or four days after the symptoms appeared. The consequences of such a pandemic were dramatic and long lasting. A shortage of farm labour drove up wages but caused output to decline, while the death of many priests through contact with their parishioners contributed to a slackening in the certainties of belief. But, in one way, the Black Death did benefit Scotland. In 1346, two years before its arrival in England, Edward III's army had defeated the Scots at the Battle of Neville's Cross, near Durham and the young king seemed set to realise his grandfather's dream of subjugating Scotland. Disease diverted him and the danger of English domination passed.

RING A RING A ROSES   A POCKET FULL OF POSIES

ATISHOO ATISHOO   WE ALL FALL DOWN

THE BLACK DEATH, DESERTED FARMS c1350s

PANEL 33 The University of St Andrews

Panel stitched by:

Elizabeth Bracher
Thelma Grieg
Kate Scorgie

Stitched in:
Kirkcaldy, Burntisland,
Kilconquhar

The oldest in Scotland and the third oldest in the English-speaking world, the university at St Andrews was formally founded by papal bull in 1413. Bishop Henry Wardlaw, commemorated in an imposing new statue near St Mary's College, had licensed a small group of teachers and students two years previously but the blessing of the papacy allowed degrees to be awarded. By the middle of the 16th century, the town, castle and university became embroiled in the Scottish Reformation and Patrick Hamilton and George Wishart were burned at the stake. By the 18th century, the university had declined and, when Samuel Johnson visited in 1773, there were only a hundred or so students. A century later, St Andrews was much strengthened by the incorporation of University College Dundee with its bias towards science and, in 1894, Agnes Blackadder graduated, becoming the first woman in Scotland to gain a similar degree to those awarded to men. Dundee became a separate university in 1967 and St Andrews was so anxious to increase its numbers in 1968 that the entrance qualifications were so low as to admit a number of unsuitable undergraduates. In 1413, Lawrence of Lindores was made rector of the university, the first in an unbroken line of distinguished rectors.

IMPREGNABLE RAMPART OF DOCTORS AND MASTERS TO RESIST HERESY

BISHOP WARDLAW

AVIGNON POPE BENEDICT XIII

ST ANDREWS UNIVERSITY 1413

PANEL 34   The Ancient Universities

Panel stitched by:

Wendy Ewart
Lindsey Fraser
Vivian French
Lesley Kerr
Elizabeth Laird
David McDowall
Vikki Reilly
Anna Renz
Kathryn Ross
Jan Rutherford
Liz Short
Gill Small
Eleanor Updale
Lesley Winton
Anna Winton

Stitched in:
West Linton, Aberdour,
Edinburgh

While England languished with only two universities, at Oxford and Cambridge, until the 18th century, Scotland had four – at St Andrews, Glasgow, Aberdeen and Edinburgh. Indeed, for a time Aberdeen had two university colleges. The historical effects of this imbalance have long been obvious. But the impulse behind these foundations is less clear. One historian has described the creation of the ancient Scottish universities as nothing less than a national programme for higher learning. But the output of graduates was small. St Andrews and Glasgow, founded in 1451, were producing perhaps only 30 graduates a year. The need to train clerics for the Reformation church certainly accelerated growth in the second half of the 16th century but what lay behind these remarkable foundations may have been something like a sense of the value of education – something that is still discernible, just, in modern Scotland. The pity is that it is now both difficult and very expensive for young people from modest backgrounds to gain entry to university and to taste something of one of Scotland's greatest cultural and historical glories.

PANEL 35 Orkney, Shetland and Scotland

Panel stitched by:

Shetland Needleworkers

Sheila Peterson
Patricia Brown
Helen Burgess
Rita Fraser
Maureen Harkness
Mali Hewamanage
Sylvia Jamieson
Juliet Nicolson

Stitched in:
Shetland

Since the Vikings began to sail 'westoversea' from Scandinavia in the eighth century, Orkney and Shetland had been under their control. Powerful Earls of Orkney such as the wonderfully named Sigurd the Stout sometimes posed a threat to the mainland. Kenneth II could do nothing to prevent Sigurd annexing Caithness and extending his reach as far south as the Moray Firth by the end of the 10th century. It was not until the 15th century that what became known as 'the matter of Norway' was resolved. In 1468, a Scottish embassy was despatched to negotiate the marriage of Margaret, the daughter of King Christian I of Denmark and Norway, to James III of Scotland. Terms were agreed and they brought to an end a long-running dispute over the payment of an annual tribute to the Scottish crown for the Western and Northern Isles. Until the full amount of Princess Margaret's dowry was paid, all of the historic rights and lands of the kings of Norway and Denmark in Orkney and Shetland were to be ceded to the Scottish crown. The dowry was never paid and, in 1472, the Northern Isles formally became part of the kingdom of Scotland. At last, the nation's frontiers reached their modern extent. And the Scandinavian character of the archipelagos began to change. The language of Norn had died out by the end of the 19th century and recent DNA studies have shown the extent of a Scottish takeover since the late 15th century. Amongst men with old Orkney surnames, such as Flett, Foubister and Linklater, Viking DNA markers are found in 35 per cent while, in the general population, it declines to only 20 per cent.

WILLIAM SINCLAIR

SCALLOWAY CASTLE

ST. NINIAN'S ISLE
TREASURE

HERRING BUSS

RAVEN CRAIG

JAMES III

MARGARET
of DENMARK

NORWEGIAN
EARLDOM of
ORKNEY

CHRISTIAN I
of DENMARK

ORKNEY AND SHETLAND
CEDED BY DENMARK TO SCOTLAND 1469

SHETLAND
Needleworkers

PANEL 36 Rosslyn Chapel

Panel stitched by:

The Apprentice Stitchers

Fiona McIntosh
Anne Beedie
Margaret Humphries
Jean Lindsay
Jinty Murray
Philippa Peat
Barbara Stokes

Stitched in:
Roslin

This gorgeously decorated and much visited chapel was founded by William Sinclair, the Earl of Orkney and Caithness, in the middle of the 15th century. Only the choir of what was intended as a family church was completed. It stands on a small hill near the dramatically sited Sinclair Castle at Roslin. The sculptural decoration of the interior is dazzling and no expense appears to have been spared in making one of the most beautiful churches in Scotland. But, after the Reformation, the chapel was closed and only reopened in 1861 under the aegis of the Scottish Episcopal Church. Many writers have attempted to make links between Rosslyn Chapel and freemasonry and the Knights Templar but none of these interpretations have so far appeared convincing. Famously, the novelist Dan Brown brought his protagonists in his *Da Vinci Code* to a denouement at Rosslyn and part of the subsequent film, starring Tom Hanks, was shot at the chapel – all of which has helped bring many thousands of visitors to an otherwise quiet corner of Midlothian.

ROSSLYN CHAPEL
A BIBLE IN STONE

PANEL 37   Chepman and Myllar

Panel stitched by:

The Bobbin Stitchers

Anne Mackinnon
Meriel Tilling

Stitched in:
Loanhead, Dalkeith

In 1507, a royal licence was granted to Walter Chepman and Andrew Myllar to print books in Scotland. For what was essentially a monopoly, the licence specified that these should be 'bukis of our lawis, actis of parliament, croniclis, mess bukis, and portuus efter the use of our Realme, with addiciouns and legendis of Scottis sanctis' and the King would decide what reasonable prices for these books should be. This seems to have been a conscious attempt at modernisation and even nation building. Sadly, the press only lasted two or three years but it did mark the beginning of a long, honourable and occasionally profitable tradition of printing and publishing in Edinburgh. Set up in the Cowgate, Chepman and Myllar did have some success and it may be that their edition of Blind Harry's *The Wallace* was a best-seller. With the *Aberdeen Breviary*, a compilation of the rituals and ceremonies of the Scottish Church intended to show how different they were from the English, the output of the new press is tinged with propaganda. But, by 1600, others had set up in business and their catalogues brimmed with popular works in Scots as well as grammars and Latin texts.

THE COMPLAINT OF THE BLACK KNIGHT   THE WALLACE   THE ABERDEEN BREVIARY   THE BUKE OF THE HOWLAT   THE GOLDEN TARGE

JOHN LYDGATE

WILLIAM DUNBAR

CHEPMAN AND MYLLAR
SET UP THE FIRST PRINTING PRESS 1507

PANEL 38 Blind Harry

Panel stitched by:

Sangstream Stitchers

Anne Rowe
Jane Angel
Sheila Capewell
Nancy Davis
Shauna Dickson
Kate Frame
Maureen Morris
Marion Mullins
Katharine Proudfoot
Gill Simpson
Donna Watt
Helen Wyllie

Stitched in:
Edinburgh

The full title of the epic poem composed by the minstrel known as Blind Harry is *The Actes and Deidis of the Illustre and Vallyeant Campioun Schir William Wallace*. It tells the tale of the great hero and royal accounts record that Harry sang 'a ballad' for King James IV on 2 January 1492 accompanied by two Gaelic clarsach players. More of a historical novel rather than a history, *The Wallace* played powerfully to patriotic sentiment and, at twelve volumes, it could not fail to make an impression. Robert Burns admired Blind Harry but others, such as the historian John Major, attacked him for inventing battles and fictional episodes in William Wallace's life. Perhaps the greatest debt is owed by Hollywood and Mel Gibson's memorable film *Braveheart*. Also ahistorical and inventive, it nevertheless excited great patriotic sentiment. Gibson also knew, as no doubt did Blind Harry, that it was principally entertainment and, when the film premiered at the Macrobert Arts Centre in the University of Stirling in 1995, the bulb in the projector blew. The star of the film leapt up onstage in his kilt and suggested he tap-danced while repairs were made. But *Braveheart* and Blind Harry's great poem both succeeded in showing just that – Wallace's extraordinary bravery.

PANEL 39 Waulking

Panel stitched by:

Wester Ross Waulkers

Liza Adam
Melinda Christmas
Lennie Cole
Isobyl la Croix
Fiona Macintyre

Stitched in:
Gairloch

For many centuries, urine was not wasted in the West Highlands or the Hebrides. It was needed for the process known as waulking cloth. Two processes were involved. The first involved scouring or removing oils and impurities from the cloth and that was where urine came in. The ammonia it contains helped in cleaning cloth. The second stage was the thickening of what had been cleaned and in Gaelic culture this gave rise to a particular music. The groups of women who sat around a table pounding and moving a bolt of cloth around would sing a very rhythmic song so that everyone worked at the same pace and in unison. Individual verses are usually sung by one person and then all join in the chorus. This last is often a string of nonsense words, the Gaelic equivalent of tra-la-la, but they can be very beguiling, almost hypnotic. '*Coisich a Ruin*', 'Come on, my love', is one of the most famous and it played to a much wider audience through the crystal voice of Karen Matheson when the band Capercaillie released a version that climbed into the UK music charts. Waulking songs are now only performed for the sake of the music since waulking itself began to be done mechanically in the 1950s.

'S MULADACH MI 'S MIR M' AINEOL

PANEL 40 Flodden

Panel stitched by:

Flodden Embroiderers

Helen De Le Mar
Caroline Proctor
Diane Skene
Belinda Trustram Eve

Stitched in:
Tongue

The reign of James IV, often seen as Scotland's first renaissance monarch, is also remembered for military disaster. In 1513, the king was killed on Flodden Field as he led the downhill charge of a large Scottish army against an English force under the command of the Earl of Surrey. It was an impulsive and foolhardy action since it removed any ability to command. Pinned in the ruck of hand-to-hand combat, James could see nothing of the course of the battle and could not affect matters once the armies had joined. By contrast, the old warrior, Surrey, stayed at the rear and was mounted so that he had some sense of where he needed to reinforce, retreat or push forward. When dawn broke on the morning after the battle, the landscape of hell was revealed. On the gently undulating northern ridge of Branxton Hill, more than 10,000 men lay dead or dying. Through a long dark night the battlefield had not been a silent graveyard. Trapped under lifeless comrades, crippled, hamstrung or horribly mutilated, fatally wounded men still breathed. Bladed weapons rarely kill outright and they were often used to bludgeon men to their knees or into unconsciousness. Some will have been put out of their misery by parties of English soldiers scouring the field by torchlight for plunder, others will have bled to death, maimed, lacerated by vicious cuts, screaming, fainting and screaming once more in their death agonies. The slaughter was unprecedented, especially thinning the ranks of the Scottish nobility, but losses were also great on the English side and no invasion of Scotland followed immediately. But Flodden ushered in a century of instability in the south – the age of the Border Reivers.

2000 ENGLISH

7000 SCOTS

JAMES IV

THE FLOOERS O' THE FOREST ARE A'WEDE AWAY

FLODDEN 1513

PANEL 41 *The Thrie Estaitis*

Panel stitched by:

The Schroders

Lynne Schroder
Jim Schroder

Stitched in:
Callander

Written by Sir David Lyndsay, this satire on the three estates of Scotland – the clergy, the nobility and the burgesses – was first performed in the open air outside Cupar in 1552. In essence an attack on these interest groups, the play was written against a background of rising tension in Scotland as the Reformation developed momentum. The Scots language used by Lyndsay is often ripe and the text contains what may be the first appearance of the word 'fuck'. It is a robust piece in another sense because its form still entertains – a production of *The Thrie Estaitis* formed the dramatic centrepiece of the 1948 Edinburgh Festival and it was adapted in 1996 by John McGrath who cast Sylvester McCoy in a major role.

PANEL 42   The Court of Session

Panel stitched by:

Mhairi MacDonald-Greig

Stitched in:
Edinburgh

In 1532, the Scottish Parliament passed an act to establish the College of Justice and it may be seen as the founding moment of the institutions of Scots law – the point at which it was made formally clear that it was different from English law. This was not the culmination of a process. Scots and English law during the Middle Ages had been largely similar. It was the outcome of a political deal. After the disaster at Flodden, James V was broke and he appealed to Pope Paul III for a portion of the Scottish church revenue that went to Rome. A sizable cut – about 10,000 gold ducats – was agreed but on one condition – Scotland had to set up a College of Justice based on the principles of canon law, complete with senators and other Roman paraphernalia. As the Reformation began to take significant hold in northern Europe, Paul III wanted to create as many institutional links as possible with Scotland. Surprisingly, these newfangled innovations survived the Scottish Reformation and, from that point on, they began to grow away from the principles of English common law. And so, for advocates, procurators fiscal and all of the other lucrative differences, we have a cash-strapped king and an astute pope to thank. When people remark that Scots law is based on Roman law, as though it adds some spurious dignity and antiquity, they should remember that it was in effect canon law. And the cost? A snip at 10,000 ducats.

PANEL 43 The Scottish Reformation

Panel stitched by:

St. Thomas's

Gladys Bennett
Audrey Axon
Alison Bogie
Sue Brown
Irene Brydon
Fiona Campbell
Wilma Finlayson
Mark Gilmour
Kay Hush
Verity Macfarlane
Margaret Mitchell
Agnes Murray
Belinda Petherick-Kerr
Mhairi Taylor
Chris Young

Stitched in:
Edinburgh

Compared with the tremendous upheavals in Europe and the blood that was spilled in France and Germany in particular, the Reformation in Scotland was relatively peaceful and quick. While there was conflict and martyrdom on both sides, a formal break with the papacy and the Catholic Church was achieved quickly. After the death of Mary of Guise, the Catholic mother of Mary, Queen of Scots, the so-called Reformation Parliament passed acts in 1560 abolishing the old faith. *The First Book of Discipline*, partly written by John Knox, set education as a priority. So that the mass of people could read the Bible, the Word of God, for themselves, there would be a school in every parish. This took much sacrifice and many years but it was eventually achieved. This set literacy in Scotland at uniquely high levels and it would form the basis of many achievements to come. But the new kirk was impoverished as secular lords and the Crown grabbed as much of the property of the old church, of the monasteries and convents as it could. The patrimony of the Dukes of Roxburgh, for example, reflects much of the estate of the Abbey of Kelso. The reformed church received only a sixth of the income of the old and even by 1562 there were only 257 ministers for 1,067 kirks. The balance was made up by more than 600 readers. John Knox is often seen as the embodiment of the Scottish Reformation as well as a by-word for dour joylessness. In reality, he was a brilliant man and a great preacher possessed of immense courage. He survived two years as a galley slave, chained to a rowing bench, to come back to Scotland to lead the forces for change.

The Word of the Lord is right and true

The Ormiston Yew

Pater noster qui es in coelis

Our Father which art in heaven

St Thomas's Church
Coffee Plus
Corstorphine

OF THE YOUTH OF THE REALM

Alison Wilma Agnes
Kay Audrey Verity
Margaret Sue Irene
Chris Fiona Belinda
Mhairi Mark Gladys

SCOTTISH REFORMATION
A SCHOOL IN EVERY PARISH, 1560's

PANEL 44 Mary, Queen of Scots

Panel stitched by:

Hopetoun Tapestry
Conservation Volunteers

Morag Austin
Margot Baird
Jane Beth Brown
Sallie Bryson
Martha Creasey
Alison Docherty
Charlotte Docherty
Ros Duffy
Gillian Gyte
Maureen Johnson
Beryl Johnston
Helen Kelly
Isobel Potts
Rita Poulter

Stitched in:
Hopetoun, Edinburgh,
Lancashire

Feckless, impulsive, romantic, beautiful, deceitful – adjectives that could all be applied to Mary, Queen of Scots. One of half a dozen instantly recognisable figures from Scottish history, she lived, reigned and was executed at a time of tremendous change – and virtually every move she made was the wrong move. The only legitimate child of James V, she succeeded to the throne at the tender age of six days. Having spent most of her childhood in France, she married the Dauphin, Francis, and, when he briefly became king, she was queen consort. On his death in 1560, Mary made plans to return to her realm of Scotland and, in 1565, she married her cousin, Henry Stuart, Lord Darnley. Two years later, he was murdered and his house at Kirk o' Field in Edinburgh blown up – probably by James Hepburn, Earl of Bothwell with whom Mary fell in love and married. After an uprising against her, Mary was forced to abdicate in favour of her son, James VI. At which point in this soap opera, she fled south to seek the protection of her cousin, Elizabeth I of England. Even though Mary had claimed her throne and was a Catholic. She was placed under stately home arrest and after eighteen and a half years in captivity, Mary was beheaded for plotting against Elizabeth. Feckless, impulsive, romantic, beautiful deceitful – and probably very unlucky, her 45 years were certainly eventful but there is a sense that the history of Scotland happened without or despite her.

SA VIRTU MATIRE

IN MY END IS MY BEGINNING

DARNLEY

BOTHWELL

FOTHERINGHAY

BATTLE OF PINKIE

AMBOISE

ROUGH WOOING

RIZZIO

VINCULA SANGUINIS ARETIORA VIRTUTIS

MA MB JB
SB AD RD
MJ ✴ BJ
HK IP GG
RP MC CD

MARY QUEEN OF SCOTS

HOPETOUN
CONSERVATORS

The Reivers and the Rescue of Kinmont Willie

Panel stitched by:

Smailholm Stitchers

Isabel Atkinson
Avril Blown
Fiona Brown
Denise Hunter
Derrick Jowett
Robyn Kinsman Blake
Susan Mason
Veronica Ross
Sally Scott Aiton
Margaret Shaw
Margaret Skea
Catherine Tees

Stitched in:
Smailholm

For almost a century after Flodden, royal authority was either weak or remote on either side of the border and a thoroughly criminalised society came into being – what is known as the age of the Border Reivers. What mattered was not the rule of law but family loyalty and, as armies crossed and recrossed the Tweed Valley or took the western route to Dumfriesshire, theft became an easier way of life than farming. Kinmont Willie Armstrong was typical. A ruthless, violent thief, he changed sides, did deals and survived. But, at a truce day in 1596, he was captured and imprisoned in Carlisle Castle. This act was in contravention of the rules of truce where those who attended cross-border hearings on complaints were immune from arrest. But the English warden, Lord Scrope, ignored this. Walter Scott of Buccleuch, on whose land Armstrong had been captured, organised a rescue. It was to be the last great raid and it was brilliantly successful – a superb example of the reivers' skills. It was the last raid because the world was about to change. Queen Elizabeth of England was old and without an heir. James of Scotland had been assured that he would succeed and no longer would thieves be able to hop over the border and play off one jurisdiction against another. The days of the Border Reivers were coming to a welcome close.

"I CURSE THAIR HEID AND ALL THE HARIS OF THAIR HEID"

DAY OF TRUCE

CARLISLE CASTLE

THE DEBATABLE LAND

THE SCOTS DYKE

LIDDESDALE

SMAILHOLM

THE CHEVIOT HILLS

TEVIOTDALE

BERWICK UPON TWEED

BLACKMAILING

THE MARCHES

BEREAVING

MY HANDS ARE TIED, BUT MY TONGUE IS FREE, AND WHAE WILL DARE THIS DEED AVOW?

THE BORDER REIVERS, RESCUE OF KINMONT WILLIE 1596

SMAILHOLM STITCHERS

PANEL 46 Robert Carey's Great Ride

Panel stitched by:

Ageing Well Edinburgh

Robina Brown
Caroline M Buchanan
Linda Garcia
Laura Kempton Smith
Kath Laing
Sheila McFarland
Sheila Miller
Mary Stewart
Ruth Watson

Stitched in:
Edinburgh

On 24 March 1603, Sir Robert Carey began a journey he hoped would bring him favour and gain. He attended the dying Queen Elizabeth in her last days and when the old queen expired, his sister, Philadelphia, pulled a ring from her finger. It had been a gift from James VI of Scotland. She gave it to her brother who rode like the wind to Edinburgh to give James the news he had been waiting for for almost 20 years. Carey had organised a relay of post horses and he reached Berwick after only 48 hours. But somewhere north of the town he fell off his horse and, while he lay on the ground, it kicked him. Spattered with blood and mud, he clattered into the inner courtyard of Holyrood-house and demanded that King James be woken. When Carey gave him the old queen's ring, he knew that his life and the history of his nation had turned in a new direction. The Union of the Crowns would surely lead to ever-closer ties. But James's new courtiers in London were not impressed with Carey. His conduct was condemned as 'contrary to all decency, good manners and respect' and he was dismissed from the post James had given him as a Gentleman of the Bedchamber. But he persisted and was eventually made Earl of Monmouth by Charles I in 1626. He wrote a memoir which became an excellent source for the story of the Border Reivers and its second edition was annotated by Sir Walter Scott.

CONTRARY
TO ALL

DECENCY
GOOD MANNERS

AND
RESPECT

RICHMOND
PALACE

25th MARCH

BEDFORD

DONCASTER

DURHAM

BERWICK
UPON TWEED

28th MARCH

HOLYROOD
PALACE

ROBERT CAREY'S RIDE FROM LONDON TO EDINBURGH 1603

PANEL 47 The Making of the King James Bible

Panel stitched by:

Heirs of 1843

Fiona Anderson
Marie Austin
Winifred Cumming
Lilias Finlay
Mary Godden
Nan Laird
Dorothy MacKenzie
Jean Mackinlay
Christine MacPhail
Deborah Miller
Elizabeth Mitchell
Maggie Morley
Jean Morrison
Judith Pickles
Maggie Romanis

with stitches from 30
members of St Andrew's
and St George's West
Church, Edinburgh

Stitched in:
Edinburgh

Begun in 1604 and completed seven years later, what is known as the King James Bible was one of the greatest achievements of his reign. Completed by 47 scholars, it set new standards of accuracy and is often hailed as the most influential piece of literature in history. Also known as the Authorised Version, it was intended to reflect the structure and particular beliefs of the Church of England. But, in truth, the brilliance of the translation from Greek for the New Testament and from Hebrew for the Old Testament has transcended that original purpose. Spelling has been modernised but the glory of the language is unaltered. Here are the first three verses from 1 Corinthians 13:

> Though I speak with the tongues of men and of angels, and have not charity, I am become as a sounding brass, or a tinkling cymbal.
> And though I have the gift of prophecy and understand all mysteries, and all knowledge, and though I have all faith, so that I could move mountains, and have not charity, I am nothing.
> And though I bestow all my goods to feed the poor, and though I give my body to be burned, and have not charity, it profits me nothing.

Vast numbers of phrases in common use come from the King James Bible as well as the text of the Lord's Prayer and the glorious translation that is Genesis 1 to 11.

A THORN IN THE FLESH

A STILL SMALL VOICE

THE ROOT OF THE MATTER

TO EVERYTHING THERE IS A SEASON

HOW ARE THE MIGHTY FALLEN

THE HOLY BIBLE CONTAINING THE OLD AND NEW TESTAMENT TRANSLATED OUT OF THE ORIGINAL TONGUES AND WITH THE FORMER TRANSLATIONS REVISED BY HIS MAJESTYS SPECIAL COMMAND

JAMES I
ENGLAND
IRELAND

JAMES VI
SCOTLAND

BY PETITION OF THE GENERAL ASSEMBLY

BURNTISLAND KIRK 1601

THE MAKING OF THE KING JAMES BIBLE 1611

HEIRS OF
1843

PANEL 48 The Dawn of the Ulster Scots

Panel stitched by:

Crewel Chicks 'n' Dave

Kate Edmunds
Shona McManus
Elizabeth Raymond
Mary Richardson
Dave Richardson

Stitched in:
Tranent, Cockenzie, Dunbar

In 1606 two ambitious Ayrshiremen launched a venture that would change the course of Irish and British history. Hugh Montgomery of Braidstane, and his near-neighbour James Hamilton from Dunlop, set up Scotland's first 'colony', across the North Channel in Ulster.

Montgomery and Hamilton both had connections at the court of King James VI/I in London. In 1605, through opportunism and influence, they managed to dispossess the Irish chieftain Con O'Neill of two-thirds of his huge landholdings in Down and Antrim. O'Neill was facing execution for alleged rebellion against the crown, and in exchange for a pardon agreed that Montgomery and Hamilton would each take one-third of his land – to be settled by Scots loyal to King James.

The following year thousands of Scots, mainly Protestant farming families from the southwest, began moving to eastern Ulster to inhabit and cultivate the lands given up by O'Neill. They and their descendants became the Ulster Scots. The success of the Hamilton/Montgomery Settlement directly inspired two further ventures blessed by King James: the Jamestown colony founded in Virginia in 1607, and the Protestant Plantation of the rest of Ulster beginning in 1610. Ulster-Scots later contributed mightily as migrants to many other countries; for example, seventeen Presidents of the United States have had Ulster Scots, or 'Scotch-Irish', ancestry.

PANEL 49 Witches

Panel stitched by:

The Coven

Jill Brennan
Val Cowan
Joan Doig
Emma Mackenzie
Elizabeth Smith

Stitched in:
North Berwick,
Athelstaneford,
East Saltoun

One of the greatest disfigurements in Scotland's history, one which banishes objectivity, was the pursuit and appalling torture and murder of women (and some men) as witches. In 1563 the interest in witchcraft stirred when the Reformation Parliament passed an act outlawing it on pain of death. By the 1590s, witch trials had begun and Agnes Sampson of North Berwick was dragged before James VI and some of his nobles at Holyrood to be interrogated. She denied all charges and was sent back to prison 'there to receive such torture as has been lately provided for witches'. Agnes was hanged by the neck, choking and vomiting for an hour before finally confessing. Her crimes were trivial and probably linked to the native tradition of folk healing and natural remedies. But the enthusiasm for such dreadful treatment was connected to the notion that Scotland was a godly commonwealth and that witches polluted it. Burning was the most common form of execution because it was seen as the most effective method of extirpating witches and witchcraft. Many women and men were strangled before fires were lit around them but others were burned alive. In Edinburgh in 1608, a group of perhaps eight women were tied to stakes to be burned alive. The fires burned through the bonds of three who ran out of the inferno with horrific burns. And the crowd threw them back in.

DUNDEE · KIRKCALDY · ORKNEY · BUTE · FORFAR
PITTENWEEM · GLASGOW · DUMFRIES · DORNOCH · AYR · SPOTT
PRESTONPANS · NORTH BERWICK · EDINBURGH · DUNKELD · ABERDEEN · BRECHIN

THOU SHALT NOT SUFFER A WITCH TO LIVE

AGNES SAMPSON

JOHN FIAN

ALISON BALFOUR · BESSIE SKEBISTER
MAGGIE OSBORNE · AGNES NAISMITH
JOHN CRAW · ANNABLE THOMSONE
MARION LILLIE · JANET HORNE

E.J.V.J-E

PANEL 50 The National Covenant

Panel stitched by:

3 in EH3

Mhairi MacDonald-Greig
Elizabeth Mason
Margo Mason
Blanka Peters

Stitched in:
Edinburgh

Signed in Greyfriars Kirkyard in 1638, this remarkable document was, in essence, a covenant between God and Scotland or Christ's Kingdom of Scotland. Many noblemen and thousands of relatively humble people attached their names, pledging themselves to defend their rights to a national church. It was a response to the efforts of Charles I to bring the church in Scotland into conformity with the Church of England. Written by Archibald Johnston and Alexander Henderson, it demanded a Scottish Parliament and a General Assembly free from royal interference and the abolition of bishops in the kirk. The Covenanters raised an army and, in what are known as the Bishops' Wars, they defeated Royalist forces. These conflicts sparked the War of the Three Kingdoms, what is usually miscalled the English Civil War. Until 1650 and the arrival of Oliver Cromwell's New Model Army, the Covenanters effectively ruled Scotland. When Charles II was restored, the Killing Times began. Covenanters were hunted down and persecuted. Unable to congregate in towns, they held field conventicles – open-air services – and sometimes thousands gathered. Covenanters were powerful in Galloway but gradually, with some lenience on offer from James II, these fiercely held beliefs died away and by the end of the 17th century only tiny sects were active.

THE NATIONAL COVENANT AT GREYFRIARS KIRKYARD 1638

PANEL 51 Droving

Panel stitched by:

The Highland Stitchers

Barbara Campbell
Agnes Greig
Penny Stevenson
Pat Thornton

Stitched in:
Muir of Ord, Culloden Moor,
Beauly

Before the transport revolutions of the 19th and 20th centuries, animals walked to market. Sheep, even geese (who were made to walk through tar and then sand so that their feet could cope with a journey) and other animals were driven to be sold but by far the greatest traffic was in cattle. The Highland economy in particular bred a tough, small breed that was in great demand to supply salt beef to the British army as the drive for empire got under way in the 18th century. Notably, drovers from Skye swam their cattle across the straits from Kylerhea to Glenelg, tying them nose to tail, before herding them through the mountain passes and down to the market known as the Falkirk Trysts. In Highland glens, particularly brilliant patches of green grass show where the stances were, the overnight stops of the herds moving through the mountains. Each summer, beasts would stop, graze and muck the ground of the stances before moving on. Rob Roy MacGregor was perhaps the most famous, or notorious, drover and it was the cattle business which caused him to become an outlaw. When the railways penetrated Scotland and the North in the later 19th century, droving came to an end. But the roads where the beasts walked can still be seen.

PANEL 52 Philiphaugh, 1645

Panel stitched by:

Ettrick & Yarrow Stitchers

Alison Blackadder
Ann Hardie
Sandra Howat
Margaret Robinson

Stitched in:
Selkirk

Having fought a brilliant campaign in the Highlands, James Graham, the Marquis of Montrose, the Royalist commander in Scotland, found himself at Philiphaugh, near Selkirk. He was pursued by a Covenanter army led by a brilliant soldier, General David Leslie, and, on 13 September 1645, plans were laid. It was misty and Montrose's scouts failed to report the advance of the enemy. The first he knew of an attack was the sound of gunfire and he arrived to find his army in some confusion. But the Royalist musketeers managed to beat off the initial assault. What Montrose did not realise was that Leslie had divided his forces and sent his cavalry along the Hartwoodburn and, screened by Howden Hill, they arrived at the battlefield and attacked the rear of the Royalist army. Brave and even reckless, Montrose charged 2,000 Covenanter dragoons with only 100 cavalry. His captains urged him to flee, telling their general that the king's cause in Scotland would be lost without him. And so, with 30 men, he cut his way out. But the cause was lost anyway and Montrose would suffer an ignominious death in Edinburgh on 21 May 1650, hanged on the Burgh Muir with a favourable biography round his neck. It was a sad end for a brilliant military tactician, a daring commander, one of several to serve the undeserving Stewart dynasty.

NEWARK CASTLE

COVENANTERS' MONUMENT

ALFORD

CHARLES I

INVERLOCHY

ETTRICK

YARROW

KILSYTH

TIPPERMUIR

1ST MARQUIS OF MONTROSE

SIR DAVID LESLIE

ABERDEEN

AULDEARN

ETTRICK & YARROW STITCHERS

MONTROSE DEFEATED AT PHILIPHAUGH NEAR SELKIRK 1645

AH SH
MR AB

PANEL 53 The Killing Times

Panel stitched by:

EH12 group

Alison Bruce, Lady Marnoch
Vivienne Cameron
Jennifer Harding-Edgar
Sue Kerridge
Steve Shillito
Leona Thomas
Chris Young

with stitches from some
members of the EAL and
other ASL services at East
Neighbourhood Centre,
Edinburgh

Stitched in:
Edinburgh

In the 1680s, the conflict between Covenanters and the government forces of Charles II and James II and VII reached its bloody crescendo. Driven out of towns and villages by powerful disapproval and the attentions of patrolling dragoons, Covenanting congregations took to the hills so that they could worship in peace. These services were known as field conventicles and sometimes thousands attended. At Irongray, near Dumfries, a huge conventicle was protected from the dragoons by a company of armed sympathisers. The Covenanting resistance to the restored Stewart monarchy's efforts to establish the Church of Scotland they wanted was at its stiffest in the south-west. At Wigtown a remarkable martyrdom took place. Passionate Covenanters, two young girls, Margaret Wilson and her sister, took to the hills to hear services and avoid persecution. But Margaret was arrested, imprisoned and, with an older woman, condemned to die a cruel death. In Wigtown Bay, they were tied to stakes at low tide and left to drown as the tide came in. As efforts to extirpate their interpretation of the Protestant faith intensified in the 1680s, Covenanters were killed or executed. Preachers were forced to go about the countryside in disguise and one of the more unlikely attempts at anonymity was the mask allegedly worn by Alexander Peden. More likely to draw attention than deflect it, the mask appears nevertheless to have been effective. In at least two places in the south of Scotland, there are rocks known as Peden's Pulpit. By the end of the 17th century, Covenanting zeal was waning – but, in contemporary Scotland, some of that thrawn spirit mercifully lives on.

PEDEN'S MASK

BASS ROCK

SKEOCH HILL

ALEXANDER McCUBINE

JOHN WELSH

JOHN DICKSON

ELSPETH ANDERSON

JAMES RENWICK

JOHN BLACKADDER

SAMUEL ARNOT

EDWARD GORDON

SDK LJT CEY JHE AB

EH12

THE KILLING TIMES IN 1680s
FIELD CONVENTICLE AT IRONGRAY NEAR DUMFRIES

PANEL 54   The Massacre at Glencoe, 1692

Panel stitched by:

Ben Nevis

Norma Callison
Sandra Casey
Karen Lees
Daphne MacLean
Johan Morton
Gillian Oram

Stitched in:
Fort William, Roy Bridge

With the departure of the Stewarts in 1688, William of Orange and his advisors kept a weather eye on the Highlands, already simmering as an area of continued support for what would be called Jacobitism. Rebellion and a victory at Killiecrankie (where the Jacobite general, John Graham, 'Bonnie Dundee', was killed) had not been followed through and resistance finally fizzled out in 1690. These events had persuaded the London government to demand oaths of allegiance in return for a pardon for any part Highland chiefs may have taken in the uprising. Many sought permission from the exiled James VII and II and, typically, he dithered. Messages of agreement were finally sent to the Highlands in the middle of December 1691. Winter snows held up Alastair MacIain, the 12th chief of the MacDonalds of Glencoe and he was late in swearing allegiance. A plot began to form. The sworn enemy of the MacDonalds, John Campbell, Earl of Breadalbane, was in London and he persuaded the Lord Advocate, John Dalrymple, the Master of Stair, that MacIain's oath was both late and not properly sworn. Stair then convinced King William to sign an order for the execution of a den of thieves in Glencoe. The massacre now had the royal seal of approval and orders were despatched north. In late January 1692, Robert Campbell of Glenlyon led 120 men into the glen where they were billeted with families. Two weeks later, probably with the arrival of fresh orders carried by a Captain Drummond, the killing suddenly began. MacIain was stabbed to death as he attempted to get out of bed and, in all, 38 men died as blades grew bloody and muskets fired. About 40 women and children subsequently perished of exposure in the snows after their houses were burned. It was a disgraceful episode but, 50 years later, much worse was to follow in the Highlands.

MASSACRE OF GLENCOE 1692

PANEL 55 The Bank of Scotland Founded

Panel stitched by:

Blacket Stitchers

Alison Cunningham
Aileen Gardiner
Jen McDowell
Roz Preston
Sue Ross Stewart
Rie Stevenson

Stitched in:
Edinburgh

In 1695, a year after the Bank of England, the Bank of Scotland was established by an act of the Scottish Parliament. It was the first in Europe to issue its own banknotes and it continues to do so. Unlike its counterpart in London, the Bank of Scotland was founded to support and finance business enterprise. Its first Chief Accountant was George Watson and a leading director was John Holland, an Englishman. Suspected of sympathy for the exiled Stewart kings, the Bank found itself in competition with an upstart rival, the Royal Bank of Scotland. It was set up by royal charter in 1727. There followed 25 years of intense competition – what were known as the Bank Wars, an enmity that has never entirely faded. Into the 20th century, mergers and acquisitions took place. The Royal Bank took over the National Commercial Bank of Scotland in 1969 and the British Linen Bank became part of the Bank of Scotland in 1971. Both had issued their own banknotes and, sadly, these fell out of circulation. In 1999, rivalry ignited once more when the Bank of Scotland attempted to take over the much larger National Westminster Bank and this prompted a bid from the Royal Bank which was ultimately successful. Throughout three centuries of business, the major Scottish banks acquired a hard-won reputation for caution and probity, for steadiness and solidity. All of which exploded in 2008 when both institutions began to fall apart in a tangle of incompetence and mismanagement. Catastrophe and immediate closure were only just averted by the prompt action of the government in guaranteeing both banks' debts. But the reputational damage will take generations to repair.

I PROMISE TO PAY THE BEARER

TAN TO UBERIOR

YESTER PAPERMILL

BANK OF SCOTLAND FOUNDED 1695

PANEL 56 The Darien Scheme

Panel stitched by:

Lasy Daisy

Liz Cameron
Lesley Evans
Margaret Lyon
Sheena MacDonald
Isobel Potts
Rita Poulter
Jean Thomson

Stitched in:
Edinburgh, Ceres

As Scotland saw its southern neighbour lay down the foundations of a great empire, the Company of Scotland was formed with the aim of fostering Scottish imperial projects. It raised a staggering sum, £400,000, about a fifth of the wealth of Scotland, in order to colonise part of the Isthmus of Panama, a place known as Darien. An original aim was to dig a canal to link the Atlantic and the Pacific. The first expedition of five ships set out from Leith in July 1698 with 1,200 people on board. Having dropped anchor in the Bay of Darien on 2 November, the settlers christened their new home Caledonia. But they were entirely unprepared for the stifling heat of the following summer, their supplies of food rotted and people began to die. The mortality rate reached ten a day. After almost a year, only 300 settlers had survived the tropical, insect-infested conditions and one ship limped back to Scotland with the terrible news. But it did not reach port in time to prevent a second expedition setting sail with a thousand hopefuls on board. Disease struck once more and the Spanish attacked the colonists' Fort St Andrew. The Darien Scheme had turned into a disaster. Of the 2,200 settlers who sailed from Scotland, only a few hundred survived and the nation lost a fortune. The episode laid a ground of failure and near-bankruptcy that pushed powerful individuals and interests closer to the idea of political – and economic – union with England.

THE DARIEN SCHEME 1698

PANEL 57 The Act of Union, 1707

Panel stitched by:

The Craiglockhart Crew

Margaret Beck
Moira Davidson
Mary Gillespie
Marysia Holmes
Maureen Johnson
Margot McDowall
Dorothy Morrison
Deborah Pearce
Margo Taylor
Alison Wardlaw
Ann Williams

Stitched in:
Edinburgh

The Darien Disaster led indirectly to the Union of the Scottish and English Parliaments. It was claimed that union would help Scotland recover. A sum of cash, known as the 'Equivalent', was paid by the English Exchequer. The amount was £398,085, almost exactly equivalent to the £400,000 lost at Darien. It was viewed as compensation by many who had invested in the scheme. From an English point of view, the deal was straightforward – they wanted to ensure that a different monarch could not reign in Scotland. By contrast, there was tremendous opposition in Scotland, especially in Edinburgh where the novelist Daniel Defoe was operating as an English spy. 'For every Scot in favour, there is 99 against!' he reported to London. But despite its unpopularity, the terms of the Act of Union were agreed in 1706 and enacted the following year. The independence of the Church of Scotland (and with it, matters of education) and the legal system were guaranteed but, in most other senses, the union was comprehensive. In addition to a unified legislature in London, there was both a customs and a monetary union. It was a hostile merger but, by the middle of the 18th century, Scotland's economy was beginning to thrive and many Scots were able to make a career in the sprawling British Empire. After the death of Queen Anne in 1714, the last of the Stewarts had gone – but their ambitions were undimmed.

THE UNITED KINGDOM OF GREAT BRITAIN

FAREWEEL TO A' OUR SCOTTISH FAME

SUCH A PARCEL OF ROGUES IN A NATION!

DUKE OF QUEENSBERRY

DUNDAS MAR SEAFIELD WEMYSS

THE ACT OF UNION. EDINBURGH, 1707

CRAIGLOCKHART

PANEL 58 The Jacobite Rising of 1715

Panel stitched by:

Dunblane Group

Judith Abbott
Heather Bovill
Caroline B Buchanan
Maud Crawford
Jenny Haldane
Mavis Oldham
Mary Storrar
Lysbeth Wilson

Stitched in:
Dunblane, Stirling,
Auchterarder

When the Act of Union of 1707 applied the Act of Settlement and assured the succession of the Protestant House of Hanover, the exiled Stewarts were compelled to act. Queen Anne, the last representative of the dynasty, had died in 1714 and George I acceded. When the Old Pretender, James Francis Edward Stuart, wrote to the Duke of Berwick in August 1715, he knew that history was waiting: 'I think it is now more than ever Now or Never.' But chronic indecision and poor communications made success ever more unlikely. Despite receiving no commission from the exiled king, John Erskine, the Earl of Mar, raised the standard of rebellion at Braemar on 27 August. Within weeks, his 12,000-strong army had control of the north and had captured Perth. Meanwhile, John Campbell, Duke of Argyll, mustered a much smaller force of 4,000 in support of George I. At Sheriffmuir, near Dunblane, the armies met and, with three times more soldiers, it looked a certain victory for Mar. But the battle was a botched, confused affair. Argyll's left wing was far shorter than the Jacobite right wing opposite them and should have been quickly outflanked, rolled up and defeated but orders were unclear. Argyll seized the initiative and, attacking the Highlanders' left wing, drove them back before turning to help his outnumbered left wing. Mar refused to commit his entire army in an all-out attack and Argyll claimed victory. A traditional song captured the confusion:

> There's some say that we wan and some say that they wan
> And some say that nane wan at a', man,
> But one thing is sure that at Sheriff Muir
> A battle was fought on that day, man,
> And we ran and they ran and they ran and we ran,
> And we ran and they ran awa' man.

KINBUCK

WHARRY BURN

SCOTS GREYS
EVANS
FORFAR
WIGHTMAN
SHANNON

MORRISON
MONTAGU
CLAYTON
KERR
CARPENTER
VOLUNTEERS
EGERTON
STAIR
ORRERY

SEAFORTH
HUNTLY
PANMURE
TULLIBARDINE
DRUMMOND
STROWAN
ANGUS

MACDONALD
FIFE
PERTH
GLENGARRY
CLANRANALD
STIRLINGSHIRE
BREADALBANE
MACLEAN
MARISCHAL

THE GATHERING STONE

13th NOVEMBER

DUKE of ARGYLL

EARL of MAR

JACOBITE RISING 1715 CHAOTIC BATTLE OF SHERIFFMUIR

PANEL 59 The Kilt

Panel stitched by:

Smailholm Group

Isabel Atkinson
Avril Blown
Fiona Brown
Denise Hunter
Derrick Jowett
Robyn Kinsman Blake
Susan Mason
Veronica Ross
Sally Scott Aiton
Margaret Shaw
Margaret Skea
Catherine Tees

Stitched in:
Smailholm, Gordon

Scottish weddings and other formal occasions now resemble a Highland Games. Within a generation, kilts – and, indeed, full tartan fig – have become de rigeur for grooms, best men and most guests. Fifty years ago Lowlanders would not have been seen dead in a kilt. The origins of all of this Highland splendour are, of course, disputed. The big kilt or plaid – a term used, confusingly, by Americans for tartan – was worn as a kilt in the modern sense but was also big enough to act as a cloak, hood or even a blanket. All was kept decent by a belt and the word kilt appears to derive from tucking in or kilting up a plaid round the waist. Many hypotheses have been advanced for the shrinking of the big kilt to the modern, small kilt. But the most likely, certainly the most entertaining, was that it was invented by an Englishman. Thomas Rawlinson was a Quaker from Lancashire who ran a charcoal burning and foundry business in Lochaber in the 1720s. Noticing that the big kilt encumbered his foresters as they felled trees and his foundry men as they smelted iron, he promoted the wearing of the small kilt. It was probably a natural development encouraged by the Englishman because illustrations of men wearing a version have been found to predate the 1720s. What was worn under the kilt remains a secret but occasionally, when Highlanders fought in hot weather, they cast off their plaids and charged in their shirts. All was on resplendent show at *Blar na Leinne*, the Field of the Shirts, a clan battle between Frasers and McDonalds near Fort William in the summer of 1544. It is not known how long the shirts were.

AND WARP WELL THE LONG THREADS, THE BRIGHT THREADS, THE STRONG THREADS, WOOF WELL THE CROSS THREADS TO MAKE THE COLOURS SHINE

FORT WILLIAM INVERNESS

INVERGARRY IRONWORKS

RIVER GARRY

MODERN KILT INVENTED LOCHABER 1723

THOMAS RAWLINSON

PANEL 60 The Jacobite Rising of 1745

Panel stitched by:

EH41

Kathleen Bain
Candy Richardson
Avis Moore
Marjory Smith
Cindy Sykes

with stitches by 32
delegates to the Episcopalian
Conference 'Ta See Oursels'

Stitched in:
Haddington

In the summer of 1745, Bonnie Prince Charlie was rowed up Loch Shiel to join the muster of his Highland army. But only a handful of men greeted him. As hopes faded, the sound of the pipes of Clan Cameron was heard. About a thousand clansmen were led to Glenfinnan by Locheil and the rising had begun. Whatever faults he had – and they appear to have been many – Charles Edward Stuart had charisma and the surprise is not that he failed but that he very nearly succeeded. Unlike the Earl of Mar and the Old Pretender, the Prince and his generals moved forward with real intent. As clansmen flocked to the standard, they moved south quickly, reaching Edinburgh in September and taking the city without loss. At Prestonpans, the Highland charge tore into the terrified ranks of a government army commanded by Sir John Cope. The battle was a rout, lasting no more than 15 minutes and Prince Charles's victory sent shock waves throughout Britain. On 8 November, the Jacobites invaded England and took Carlisle. But, by the time they reached Derby, the three government armies in England were closing in. Even if the Highlanders won again, they would lose between 1,000 and 1,500 casualties and that would make a fighting retreat back to Scotland impossible. Meanwhile London was in uproar, the stock market was falling and nervous preparations were made. The argument for retreat prevailed and it led all the way to Culloden and defeat in April 1746. The Stewart cause was at last lost. It was the beginning of a long end for the clans and an appallingly punitive campaign of killings and rapes followed the departure of the Prince. He died drunk, dissolute and friendless in Italy.

PRINCESS MARIA

In Memorium

In Memorium

OLD PRETENDER

THE YOUNG PRETENDER

ERISKAY

BORRODALE

GLENFINNAN

PRESTONPANS

DERBY

CULLODEN

ARISAIG

JACOBITE ROSE

ROSA ALBA

PRINCE'S STANDARD

FLORA McDONALD

The little gentleman in the velvet jacket

HADDINGTON

KING'S TOAST

JACOBITE RISING 1745

Kathleen

PANEL 61 The Ordnance Survey

Panel stitched by:

Inverness & Area

Judie Holliday
Anne Omand

Stitched in:
Fortrose, Dochgarroch

One of the reasons the Jacobite army penetrated as far south as Derby in 1745 was the lack of good mapping and decent roads. The far superior government forces were unable to react, to move quickly enough to position themselves and their artillery in the path of a fast-moving Highland army. That is why the wonderfully detailed and accurate maps of Britain are called the Ordnance Survey. In 1747, Lt Col. David Watson proposed that reliable maps of the Scottish Highlands be made to ensure that rebellious clansmen could not simply disappear into an uncharted wilderness or use local geographical knowledge to tactical advantage. The resulting maps were scaled on one inch to a thousand yards. War, or the threat of war, stimulated the mapping of the South of England when William Roy, one of Watson's assistants in Scotland, began to work on Kent and Sussex. Fear of a French invasion was the prompt. By the 1820s, the first complete surveys of England and Wales were produced. The Ordnance Survey is an adornment to life in Britain, despite the recent abandonment of the green Pathfinder series, a set of superbly detailed maps easily handled out of doors. By comparison, maps of European countries are poor but, during the First World War, the Ordnance Survey began work on maps of Belgium, France and Italy. Would that they were more easily available.

THE ORDNANCE SURVEY BEGINS

PANEL 62 English Advances, Gaelic Retreats

Panel stitched by:

In Stitches

Jean Gowans
Tina Hammond
Carolyn Irvine of Drum
Helen Jackson
Diana Munro
Mairi Skinner

Stitched in:
Banchory, Letham, Potarch

The defeat at Culloden in 1746 was the beginning of a long end for the Highland clans, their culture and their language. Gaelic had crossed the North Channel from Ireland with the establishment of the kingdoms of Dalriada and, at its zenith, the language was spoken all over the Highlands and the Western Isles but, as the brutal aftermath of the Jacobite Risings merged into the Clearances, people left the Highlands with Gaelic, a language that they rarely passed on to their children. Now it is spoken by less than 1 per cent of all Scots. The original native tongue of Scotland was what might be best described as Old Welsh or Cumbric. Now entirely effaced, its only traces are to be found in the landscape, in natural features and place names. Peebles is from *pebyll*, the Old Welsh word for tents and it probably meant a shieling. Altcluit meant the Rock of the Clyde, now Dumbarton Rock, and Penicuik is from *Pen y Cog*, Cuckoo Hill. Early versions of English invaded with the Angles as they overran the Tweed Basin and the Lothians in the seventh century and, in the medieval period, it spread with the establishment of towns and trade. But, until the 19th century, Gaelic reached down the Perthshire, Angus and Aberdeenshire glens and it is likely that those who lived on either side of the linguistic frontier understood each other well enough. Now the fate of Gaelic is very perilous and, if it is lost, it will be all Scotland's loss.

ACT OF PROSCRIPTION
1747

OBAIR DHEATHAIN ABERDEEN

GLASCHU GLASGOW

DUN EIDEANN EDINBURGH

DUN DEAGH DUNDEE

PEAIRT PERTH

INBHIR NIS INVERNESS

AN EAGLAIS BHREAC FALKIRK

WADE'S ROAD

JAMES STEWART   AIRTS AND PAIRTS

APIN MURDER   1752

ENGLISH ADVANCE GAELIC RETREAT

PANEL 63 The Royal and Ancient Golf Club

Panel stitched by:

Tee'd Off

Pat Freeth
Jennifer Link
Eddie Link
Shona Morrison
Lis Smith
Sheila Tunstall-James
Mairi Wheeler

Stitched in:
Kinross, Glenlomond,
Auchtermuchty,
Forgandenny, St Monans

Golf is a Scottish invention. All other claims are entirely insubstantial and at St Andrews and around Edinburgh the modern game began to take shape. The Royal and Ancient Golf Club of St Andrews is probably not the oldest in the world. That honour could probably be claimed by the Royal Burgess Golfing Society of Edinburgh which was founded almost 20 years before, in 1735. But the R&A is the most powerful because it makes the rules. But it does not own a golf course. The Old Course and the others around it are the property of the citizens of the town of St Andrews. Regarded as the home of golf, the links (i.e. seaside) courses are also closest to the game's origins. The strip of land behind the dunes of the West Sands, what is now the world-renowned Old Course and its sister courses, was too sandy for cultivation and was used for grazing. In the bitter winter winds, sheep scraped out bields or shelters and these sandy indentations became known as bunkers. The fairways of the Old Course were not laid out or created but are the well-mown folds of naturally undulating land. And the rough is very rough. On a calm summer's day, the Old Course seems to present few difficulties to the professionals who contend for the Open Championship. But, when the wind blows, it becomes evil, unfair, impossible – a conspiracy of nature and the R&A. In reality the Old is the greatest golf course in the world. Bar none.

BAILLIE WILLIAM LANDALE

THE HONORABLE COMPANY OF EDINBURGH GOLFERS

GENTLEMEN GOLFERS OF LEITH

ROYAL AND ANCIENT GOLF CLUB FOUNDED IN ST ANDREWS 1754

The First School for Deaf and Dumb Children

Panel stitched by:

Cammo Quilters

Katherine Forsyth
Rosemary Gordon-Harvey
Avril Green
Elizabeth Reekie
Gillian Swanson
Norma Watkins
Caroline Watson

Stitched in:
Edinburgh

Thomas Braidwood founded the first school in Britain designed to teach deaf and dumb children. It was set up in a house in the Canongate in Edinburgh in 1780. Developing out of what he called the 'combined system', Braidwood codified the earliest version of British Sign Language. It was based on the use of the hands, the shapes they made, how they were turned, were placed and moved. C is made by curving the thumb and index finger into a semicircle and D by adding the straight index finger of the other hand to the semicircle. Deaf and dumb people talk in a mesmerising flurry of hand movements and British Sign Language has developed regional dialects. Some Scottish signs are not understood in the south of England. Braidwood's first pupil was Charles Sheriff, the son of Alexander Sheriff, a wealthy wine merchant working in Leith. The school tended to cater for those with the means to pay its fees but Joseph Watson, a relative of Braidwood, founded the first public school for the deaf and dumb. Based in Bermondsey in 1792, the London Asylum for the Deaf and Dumb was very successful. By 1783, Braidwood himself had moved to London to found a new school and his grandson set up a school in Virginia in the USA. Scots pioneered this field of education and Thomas Braidwood would have smiled to see British Sign Language recognised alongside English, Welsh, Gaelic and others as one of Britain's official languages and also to see that his original school in the Canongate is remembered in the nearby district of Edinburgh, the Dumbiedykes.

DUMBIEDYKES

THOMAS BRADWOOD

DUMBIE HOUSE

CHARLES SHERIFF

ALEXANDER SHERIFF

FIRST SCHOOL FOR DEAF AND DUMB CHILDREN
ESTABLISHED IN EDINBURGH 1760

James Small and the Swing Plough, 1770

Panel stitched by:

Christine Covell
Sandra Douglas
Linda Jobson

Stitched in:
Peebles, Eskbank

Scottish agriculture had long been hampered by poor technology. The Auld Scots Ploo was built mostly of wood tipped by iron and it took a team of four powerful oxen to pull it through the ground. It often broke down when it hit big stones or roots. And because it did not turn the sod completely, the auld ploo needed an army of plough followers to break up big clods and pull out weeds. In the 1770s, a Berwickshire blacksmith, James Small, perfected the swing plough. Cast all in iron at the Carron Ironworks, it had a screwed shape that turned the sod over completely, could be pulled by one strong horse and guided by one skilled man. Because it ploughed a deeper furrow, the swing plough improved drainage and brought more land into cultivation. Small was a perfectionist who worked on his prototypes endlessly and even spent time in prison as a debtor. He did not patent his design and consequently it was imitated very widely. This in turn accelerated the speed of change on the land and its adoption on the prairies of the USA and Canada made these regions into the breadbaskets of the world. Even now James Small is little known and his huge contribution to the modern world badly understood. He died in 1793 of overwork and in great poverty. The swing plough changed cultivation radically and, by doing that, it changed the world.

BLACKADDER MOUNT

TREATISE ON PLOUGHS AND WHEEL CARRIAGES 1784

I SHALL NOT PROFIT FROM MY INVENTION

CARRON WORKS

JAMES SMALL INVENTS THE SWING PLOUGH 1770

CHRISTINE

PANEL 66 Enlightenment Edinburgh

Panel stitched by:

Shepherd House Group

Jean Cameron
Ann Fraser
Sarah Hynd
Marianne More Gordon
Frances Stevens

Stitched in:
Inveresk, Musselburgh,
North Berwick

Perhaps the most glittering period in Scotland's history was the second half of the 18th century – what is known as the Enlightenment. Between 1768 and 1771, Encyclopaedia Britannica was established in Edinburgh by William Smellie, a printer, editor and antiquary. At Anchor Close, just off the High Street, work began on setting down all human knowledge – it was an age when such a feat was thought possible, the organisation of all there is to know. The Encyclopaedia appeared in 100 weekly instalments and could be pithy. The entry for Woman was four words long – 'the female of man'. But it proved popular and a second edition was soon put in train. It was published at a time of great intellectual ferment in Scotland and in Edinburgh in particular. An English visitor, a chemist called Amyat, left a famous observation, 'Here I stand at what is called the Cross of Edinburgh [the Mercat Cross in the High Street] and can, in a few minutes, take 50 men of genius and learning by the hand.' It was an intense environment. The medieval tenements of the Old Town piled people on top of each other and intellectual clubs met to discuss and dispute in the taverns off the High Street and the Canongate. The Select Society was founded by the painter Allan Ramsay, and the philosophers David Hume and Adam Smith. The Poker Club was intended to 'poke things up a bit'. Publishing was busy but this remarkable period of intellectual achievement was underpinned and understood by a society where, at 75 per cent, mass literacy was the highest in the world.

NEWHAILES HOUSE

BALLOON TYTLER

ANDREW BELL

ENGRAVINGS

WILLIAM SMELLIE

COLIN MACFARQUHAR

ANDREW BELL

ENLIGHTENMENT EDINBURGH, ENCYCLOPAEDIA BRITANNICA
ESTABLISHED AT ANCHOR CLOSE 1771

Shepherd House Group

PANEL 67 Edinburgh's New Town

Panel stitched by:

Catherine Harlick

Stitched in:
Rhiconich

Overcrowding and building collapse forced the city council to extend Edinburgh's boundaries to include the farmland beyond the Nor Loch, an unpleasant body of water that lay at the northern foot of the Castle Rock. It is now Princes Street Gardens. A design competition for what would be known as the New Town was won by 26-year-old James Craig and his simple layout of a grid of three main streets linking two squares and crossed by five north-to-south thoroughfares is essentially what survives today. The street and square names reflected contemporary politics. George Square and St Andrew Square were to represent the union of the two nations. But someone remembered that there was already a George Square on the south side of the city and so Queen Charlotte was commemorated in Charlotte Square as well as Queen Street. And the royal princes were immortalised in Princes Street, although few can remember their names. Intended as a residential suburb, the New Town has a very pleasing symmetry. There were problems at each end in the south which were never quite resolved. Craig intended George Street to have a church in the squares at each end to finish the vistas but Sir Lawrence Dundas decided to build his house in St Andrew on the site intended for the church and St Andrew and St George's is in George Street. The connection with the Old Town down the Mound was not properly planned, resulting in the chicane into Hanover Street but perhaps the most glaring misfit is Queensferry Street and the way it is awkwardly attached to the south side of Charlotte Square and the west end of Princes Street. But the whole scheme is a wonderfully harmonious and concrete testament to the Edinburgh Enlightenment and a time when the city council could get things right.

PANEL 68   James Watt and the Steam Engine

Panel stitched by:

Campsie Stitchers

Nancy Bailey
Isobel Shaw
Jacky Young

Stitched in:
Glasgow

Born in Greenock in 1736, James Watt became a distinguished engineer and inventor – a Scot whose fame remains worldwide. But he did not invent the steam engine – rather, he made it work much more efficiently. While employed at Glasgow University as an instrument maker, Watt saw how wasteful of energy designs for steam engines were. They repeatedly cooled and reheated their cylinders. Instead, Watt invented the separate condenser and this hugely improved the power and efficiency of pumps in particular. And it made them cheaper to manufacture. When Watt conceived a means of producing rotary motion, the use of the steam engine broadened well beyond pumping. The brilliance of what he achieved could be seen on old steam trains where the huge iron wheels were very obviously driven by rotary power. In partnership with Matthew Boulton, Watt became a wealthy man and, throughout his life, he continued to work on inventions. Not only did he come up with the concept of horsepower as a means of measurement, the unit of electricity known as a watt is named after him.

JOSEPH BLACK

HAMMERMEN

$W = \dfrac{NKm}{S}$

CARRON WORKS

VIA VERITAS VITA

UNDERWOOD MILL PAISLEY

THOMAS TELFORD

WILLIAM MURDOCH

CRAIGELLACHIE

INNOVATION

STEVENSON BELL ROCK

CAMPSIE STITCHERS

NANCY BAILEY ISOBEL STRANG JACKY TONNER

JAMES WATT AND THE STEAM ENGINE

PANEL 69 The Tobacco Lords

Panel stitched by:

The Last Gasp Group

Marie Abbott
Jenny Barnett
Sheila Bruges
Elma Muir
Sally Nairn
Anne North
Pamella Roberts
Hilda Stewart

Stitched in:
Blairgowrie, Perth, Dunkeld

The Act of Union may have been deeply unpopular in Edinburgh but it converted Glasgow into a very busy port. Its position on the Clyde was enormously important in the age of sailing ships. The trade winds first hit Europe in the west of Scotland and this gave ships sailing out of Glasgow for the American colonies a two-to-three-week advantage. From 1710 until c. 1760, the city boomed because of the trade in tobacco. The wealthiest and most enterprising merchant was John Glassford and he ran a fleet of 25 merchant ships. Known as the Tobacco Lords or sometimes the Virginia Dons, Glasgow merchants built huge mansions that gave their names to the city's streets – Thomas Buchanan, Archibald Ingram and Glassford amongst them. The American Revolution of 1776 caused great difficulties. The Glasgow merchants had lent vast sums to the planters of Virginia and Maryland and, after the break with Britain, few of these debts were ever repaid. But, ever versatile, the Tobacco Lords switched their trade to cotton in the British West Indies. Their most lasting legacy is in Glasgow's Georgian architecture.

PANEL 70 Adam Smith

Panel stitched by:

Meg Murray
Christine Simm
Jean Taylor
Fiona Wemyss
Dorie Wilkie
Fiona Wilkie

Stitched in:
Forgandenny, Edinburgh

Perhaps the most influential thinker of the Scottish Enlightenment, Adam Smith was born in Kirkcaldy in 1723. The old harbour fascinated him as he watched ships load and unload at the quaysides. Having studied at Glasgow University and Oxford, he lectured at Edinburgh before being appointed Professor of Moral Philosophy at Glasgow. He is rightly renowned for two enormously influential pieces of scholarship. *The Theory of Moral Sentiments* was published in 1759 but the work he is most famous for is *An Inquiry into the Nature and Causes of the Wealth of Nations*. It is considered the first modern treatment of economics and it has been enormously influential since its publication in 1776. Many scholars see Smith's dictum of the play of self-interest in economic life as being summarised in this famous sentence:

> It is not from the benevolence of the butcher, the brewer or the baker, that we expect our dinner, but from their regard to their own interest. We address ourselves, not to their humanity but to their self-love, and never talk to them of our own necessities but of their advantages.

As with many great thinkers, Smith has been interpreted by politicians of many different persuasions but his clear-eyed thinking makes his work highly accessible almost 250 years after *The Wealth of Nations* was first published.

THE INVISIBLE HAND

OLD HARBOUR

ADAM SMITH THE WEALTH OF NATIONS KIRKCALDY

David Hume and Jean-Jacques Rousseau

Panel stitched by:

Coastal Stitchers

Sheila Baird
Jean Dawson
Christina Dougan
Alison Sanchez-Ruiz
Esther Sharpley
Hilary Williams

Stitched in:
Aberlady, Ballencrieff,
Gullane

Famously decent and mild-tempered, the great philosopher of the Edinburgh Enlightenment David Hume was known as Le Bon David. This title was conferred on him in Paris where he acted as the under-secretary to the British ambassador, Lord Hertford, between 1763 and 1765. He was lionized for his work, writing to a fellow historian that 'I can only say that I eat nothing but ambrosia, drink nothing but nectar, breathe nothing but incense and tread on nothing but flowers'. This idyll was disturbed by the case of the philosopher, Jean-Jacques Rousseau. After the publication of his radical tract, *The Social Contract*, with its famous first line, 'Man is born free and everywhere he is in chains', he was persecuted. Hume offered to take Rousseau to safety in England despite warnings that the refugee was not a man to be trusted. And they soon quarrelled. Rousseau suspected a plot against him and began to abuse him and draw friends and influential people into the row. In less than a year, their relationship had descended into mutual loathing. Such was Hume's fury that his reputation for moderation and goodness was severely endangered when he wrote of Rousseau as 'surely the blackest and most atrocious villain, beyond comparison, that now exists in the world'. Oh dear.

THE POKER CLUB.

1762.

JOHN KAY

OYSTER LASS

HUME ON HUMAN NATURE

1739

ÉMILE

LE BON DAVID.

COUNTESS DE BOUFFLERS

SULTAN.

THE SELECT SOCIETY

1754

DAVID HUME AND JEAN-JACQUES ROUSSEAU IN PARIS.

The Highland and Lowland Clearances Gather Pace

Panel stitched by:

Links Needlework

Susie Alexander
Betty Beazley
Isabel Bryce
Margaret Cormack
Helen Deasy
Sheena Esson
Liz Farmer
Edwina Fraser
Lynn Fraser
Sheena Fraser
Cath Fraser
Margaret Gowans
Ada Grant
Kathleen Grant
Marion Hailstone
Sheila Hamilton
Cath Hay
Stephanie Hoyle
Cathy MacGillivray
Janet Mackenzie
Anne Marie Mackenzie
Margaret MacLennan
Evelyn Main
Mary McBean
Mairi Neilan
Evelyn Reid
Ann Sutherland
Dorothy Sutherland
Ingrid Wallace
Mary Williams

Stitched in:
Nairn

In the late 18th and throughout the 19th century, both the Highlands and Lowlands of Scotland slowly emptied of people. Landlords wanted to make profits from sheep or sporting estates and, in the Lowlands, smallholders were cleared as farms grew larger and more cost-effective. The growing cities of the Central Belt offered work for many but significant numbers reached the quaysides of Glasgow, Greenock and elsewhere and kept going, seeking new lives in North America, Australia, New Zealand and other developing countries. It may be that the Highland Clearances are better understood because of the actions of what seemed like a brutal aristocracy. There was resistance and, at the Battle of the Braes in Skye in 1882, crofters fought with the police. But the Napier Commission met and a reform of the law allowed security of tenure and limited the ability of landlords to evict families.

BARNS NESS

SKATE RAW RIDGE

FATHER OF MODERN GEOLOGY

"NO VESTIGE OF A BEGINNING, NO PROSPECT OF AN END."

UNCONFORMITY

PLAYFAIR   HALL   HUTTON

SICCAR POINT

SALISBURY CRAGS

HUTTON'S ROCK

HAWK'S HEUGH

PEASE BAY

COVE

N
W   E
S

BARNS NESS
SKATERAW
TORNESS POINT
THORNTONLOCH
DUNGLASS
COVE
HAWK'S HEUGH
PEASE BAY
SICCAR POINT
FAST CASTLE
EAST LOTHIAN
SICCAR POINT
BERWICKSHIRE

MARY R.
KATE E.
SHONA M.
ELIZABETH R.
'n' DAVE

JAMES HUTTON'S THEORY OF THE EARTH,
SICCAR POINT, BERWICKSHIRE

CREWEL CHICKS
'n' DAVE

PANEL 75 James Boswell and Smoked Fish

Panel stitched by:

The Coburg Ladies

Catherine Aitken
Sarah McCabe
Margaret McCabe
Annie Wright

Stitched in:
Prestonpans

In the late 18th century, James Boswell gained a literary reputation as the biographer and companion of Dr Samuel Johnson but he also had something to say about Finnan haddies. Being very partial to the lightly smoked haddock from the village of Findon, near Aberdeen, Boswell was pleased to see them available in London but less happy when he tasted them. So that they made the sea journey unspoiled, the Finnan haddies had been much more heavily smoked and were, frankly, a bit tough. Arbroath smokies are the other famous product of the east coast. Also haddock, they are first salted overnight and then tied in pairs with hemp twine. Left to dry, they are hung over a triangular piece of wood and set over a fire of hardwood in a barrel. This is then sealed with a wet jute sack (so that it won't catch fire) and within only an hour, the haddocks are cooked. A beautiful rich brown, Arbroath smokies are a genuine delicacy – although not delicate but strong-tasting. Boswell's views are not recorded – nor do they matter a jot.

The Forth and Clyde Canal, Burke and Hare

Panel stitched by:

Whippity Stouries

Christine Simm
Jean Taylor
Fiona Wilkie

Stitched in:
Bo'ness

James Hutton's investment in a canal linking the east and west of Scotland was worthwhile and, in the early 19th century, work began on digging a canal between Fountainbridge in Edinburgh and Port Dundas in Glasgow. The men doing the labouring work were known as navigators or navvies and many of these were Irish. The most notorious were William Burke and William Hare who committed a series of unusual murders in 1828, the details of which were very memorable. They sold the corpses of their 16 victims to Dr Robert Knox, an anatomist at Edinburgh University who needed fresh bodies for dissection. He charged fees for his lectures and, although he was never arrested or brought to trial, the Edinburgh mob and the press believed that Knox was complicit in the murders. When Burke was convicted and sentenced to death (Hare turned King's evidence and was granted immunity from prosecution), the judge specified that his body be publicly dissected. This famous case did not spark any anti-Irish rioting but it did spawn many films, TV programmes, plays, novels and songs.

THE FORTH AND CLYDE CANAL
IRISH NAVVIES, BURKE AND HARE

PANEL 77 Scotland and the Drive for Empire

Panel stitched by:

The Meikle Family

Graham Meikle
Fiona Meikle
Annabel Meikle

Stitched in:
Pathhead, Edinburgh

As the British Empire expanded in the second half of the 18th century, Scots were at the forefront. Out of all proportion to the relative populations, there were many Scots serving in the British Army, especially Highlanders. Sorely in need of troops to prosecute the Seven Years War against the French, the Prime Minister, William Pitt, encouraged the recruitment of two regiments of clansmen. Justifying putting arms into the hands of men who had rebelled against the crown only ten years before, Pitt wrote to the king, saying:

> I sought for merit wherever it was to be found. It is my boast that
> I was the first minister who looked for it and found it in the
> mountains of the north. I called it forth and drew into your service
> a hardy and intrepid race of men . . . [T]hey served with fidelity
> as they fought with valour and conquered for you in every part
> of the world.

The last Highland charge was probably made at the battle for control of Canada on the Heights of Abraham. Much of the British Empire was bought by the blood of the clans. More peacefully, Scots became involved centrally in the East India Company, especially after it came under the control of Henry Dundas. Many Orcadians in particular worked in Canada for the Hudson's Bay Company as it opened up the vast interior of the north. And what cannot be ignored is the involvement of many Scots in the infamous triangular trade. Merchant ships took manufactured goods to West Africa where they were traded for slaves. They were then shipped in 'the middle passage' to the Caribbean and to the USA where so-called cash crops such as sugar, rum, molasses, tobacco, hemp and cotton were loaded for the return voyage to Britain.

SCOTLAND AND THE DRIVE FOR EMPIRE

PANEL 78 Robert Owen and New Lanark

Panel stitched by:

New Lanark

Lea Barrie
Susan Finlayson
Janice Glover
Nancy Howat
Tamara Jones
Julia McMurray
Lesli Paterson
Marjorie Romer
Pat Strong
Liz Young

with stitches by members of
the New Lanark Trust staff

Stitched in:
Lanark, Glasgow

A child of the Enlightenment, Robert Owen was a mill manager in Manchester who became interested in the welfare of his workers. During a visit to Glasgow, he fell in love with Caroline Dale, the daughter of David Dale, the owner of the mills at New Lanark. The mills there derived their power from the Falls of the Clyde. Owen persuaded his partners to buy New Lanark and he proceeded to make a series of reforms. First he opened a mill shop for his workers that sold quality goods at little more than wholesale prices and, when bulk buying created profits, these were passed on to customers. These principles became the basis for the Co-op. Owen also founded infant childcare at New Lanark and promoted the education of the children of his workers. After a time, Owen's mind turned to more political and philosophical activities. He began to lobby for changes in legislation but was unhappy with the Factory Act of 1819. Owen wrote *The Revolution in the Mind and Practice of the Human Race* in which he argued that character is formed by nature and individual circumstances. By 1828, after some disagreements, Owen resigned all connection with New Lanark and, based in London, he formed the Association of all Classes of all Nations and it was he who coined the term 'socialism'.

WORLD HERITAGE

ATLANTIC

abc

ROBERT OWEN

COTTON

DAVID DALE

NEW LANARK 1785

PANEL 79 Robert Burns and 'Tam o' Shanter'

Panel stitched by:

Blister Sisters

Mary Doherty
Maureen Finlay
Margaret Mitchell
Margaret Potter

Stitched in:
East Calder

The genius of Robert Burns lay in his ability to create poetry that is complex, tremendously beautiful and accessible to all. At Burns Suppers the world over, the recital, usually from memory, of 'Tam o' Shanter' is a highlight. Pure entertainment, it is probably one of the most rollicking, energetic poems ever composed. Written in 1790, the poem first appeared a year later in the *Edinburgh Magazine* before being published in Francis Grose's *Antiquities of Scotland*. Burns asked Grose to include a drawing of Alloway Kirk and Grose agreed so long as the poet wrote something to go with it. The glorious result was 'Tam o' Shanter'. The opening is unmatched:

> When chapman billies leave the street,
> And drouthy neibors, neibors meet;
> As market days are wearing late,
> And folk begin to tak the gate,
> While we sit bousing at the nappy,
> An' getting fou and unco happy,
> We think na on the lang Scots miles,
> The mosses, waters, slaps and stiles,
> That lie between us and our hame,
> Where sits our sulky, sullen dame,
> Gathering her brows like gathering storm,
> Nursing her wrath to keep it warm.

ROBERT BURNS' TAM O'SHANTER 1791

PANEL 80 The False Alarm

Panel stitched by:

Lady Stitchers

Sonya Anderson
Phyllis Hogg
Barbara Plevin

Stitched in:
Broxburn, Port Seton

As the French invasion force assembled at Boulogne in 1803–04, Napoleon itched to add Britain to his conquests but the weather was against him. Nevertheless, the threat was taken very seriously and nowhere more so than in the Scottish Borders. The old early warning system used in the days of English invasion was revived as balefires were piled up on hills and high points. If the French landed on the North Sea coast, a relay of beacons would be lit and the forces of volunteers recruited in the countryside would muster. Walter Scott, attached to the Midlothian Yeomanry Cavalry, was amongst these. On 31 January 1804, the system went spectacularly into action. A volunteer sergeant new to the Borders peered into the darkness from the balefire at Hume Castle and, yes, he was certain he could make out the yellow flames of a fire lit on Dowlaw in north Northumberland. Having lit the Hume balefire, the alarm crackled rapidly through the Borders as beacons were lit on Peniel Heugh, the Dunion and Crumhaugh Hill at Hawick. These triggered others to be lit in Teviotdale, Ettrick and Yarrow. When volunteers saw the fires, adrenalin must have pumped as they pulled on their boots and buckled on their sabres. Walter Scott was in Cumberland when the Hume bale was fired and he rode 100 miles to join his regiment at Dalkeith. The Borders was in uproar and rumours ricocheted. Regiments of Napoleon's cuirassiers were expected to come clattering along the Berwick road at any moment. But they did not. No one did. What the unfortunate sergeant at Hume had seen was not a balefire but the everyday work of some Northumbrian charcoal burners. Phew.

WISP

CRUM HAUGH

31ST JANUARY

BELLING HILL

EILDON HILL

RUBERS LAW

3000 VOLUNTEERS

PENEIL HEUGH

DUNION HILL

HUME CASTLE

DALKEITH MELROSE SELKIRK HAWICK

ST BOSWELLS KELSO JEDBURGH

THE FALSE ALARM THREAT OF NAPOLEONIC INVASION 1801

SKA. BAP

SKA. BAP

PANEL 81 Henry Raeburn

Panel stitched by:

Jennifer Myles

Stitched in:
South Queensferry

The Rev. Robert Walker's day out skating on Duddingston Loch was immortalised by Henry Raeburn in the 1790s. It was only one stunning portrait from many painted by, arguably, Scotland's first great master. In a busy life, he produced hundreds of superb works, amongst them beautifully observed portraits of Walter Scott and Alastair Ranaldson Macdonell of Glengarry. These two illustrate Raeburn's great subtlety. A handsome man and one of the most famous people in Europe during his lifetime, Scott liked to portray himself as a straightforward sort of man. But, with a wonderful handling of light and the ability to capture expression, Raeburn shows an altogether more complex man, with sadness as well as creativity seeming to emanate from his gaze into the middle distance. Macdonell of Glengarry was a well-known clan chief and he was the model for Scott's creation, Fergus Mac-Ivor in his first novel, *Waverley*. Dressed in full Highland fig and clutching a musket, he looks the very epitome of the clansman whose genealogy and history reach back into the mists of time. But his features and expression are telling. He was known as a haughty and ruthless man. Far from being the protector of his people, he cleared Glengarry of crofters, felled timber for sale and exploited his patrimony for his own profit. Such is the quality and variety of Raeburn's portraits between the 1790s and 1820s that they can be read as a commentary on the age.

PANEL 82 Walter Scott

Panel stitched by:

Catherine Guiat
Eileen Henderson
Annette Hunter

Stitched in:
Edinburgh

Scott was a phenomenon – a figure who helped form many perceptions of modern Scotland. Born in Edinburgh in 1771, he was educated to follow his father into the law but Scott's lameness, perhaps caused by a bout of polio, sent him to recuperate in the Borders with relatives. These visits influenced the 'wee sick laddie' very much. At his grandparents' farm near Kelso, he listened to his aunt recite the Border ballads and they fired his imagination. As a young man, he began to make written copies of the ballads, what had been mainly an oral tradition. In 1802 and 1803, Scott had published *The Minstrelsy of the Scottish Border* and the three volumes were very successful. But, in 1805, this collection was spectacularly overshadowed by Scott's own composition, *The Lay of the Last Minstrel*. This long narrative poem, set in the Borders, became a huge best-seller and it established the author as a figure of real renown. He brought out two more long poems, *Marmion* and *The Lady of the Lake*. With his novel *Waverley* and a string of subsequent successes, Scott became a worldwide name, the first author to be feted during his own lifetime. His novels also turned Scotland into a destination for tourists, especially when the railways came after the 1860s. And his fame had all sorts of other effects. When Scott organised the state visit of George IV to Scotland, he wrapped it in tartan, making the whole thing a Highland affair. This, in turn, caused the Borders textile mills to clack and rattle as demand for tartan boomed. Tragically, a series of unhappy business deals impoverished Scott and he killed himself with overwork to pay back his debts.

SHERIFF OF SELKIRK

MALACHI MALAGROWTHER

WAVERLEY

IVANHOE

ROB ROY

THE LADY OF THE LAKE

THE HEART OF MIDLOTHIAN

SCOTT'S VIEW

GEORGE IV VISIT TO SCOTLAND 1822

CG EH AH

WALTER SCOTT, EARLY 19th CENTURY,
ROMANTIC SCOTLAND AND THE BEGINNINGS OF TOURISM

MAIDA

PANEL 83 Fingal's Cave

Panel stitched by:

Scoraig Stitchers

Alison Barr
Jill Beavitt
Aggie Brudenell
Kath Bush
Catherine Dagg
Anthea Douglas
Agnes Greig
Nick Lancaster
Joany McGuire
Susan McSweeney
Jessie Millard
Hugh Piggott
Djinni Van Slyke

Stitched in:
Dundonnell

James Macpherson had style – or, at least, nerve. In 1760, he was induced to have published *Fragments of Ancient Poetry Collected in the Highlands of Scotland*, a set of translations he claimed to have made from Gaelic. A year later, he announced the discovery of something astonishing, something to rival the classical epics of Homer and Virgil. Composed by Ossian, at some time in the distant and mist-strewn past, this was *Fingal, an Ancient Epic Poem in Six Books*. Wildly popular and deeply suspect at the same time, the work of Ossian/Macpherson helped create a vision of a romantic Highlands where a noble past had created tales to rival anything in Latin and Greek. Goethe adored the poems and Napoleon reputedly kept a copy by him on campaign. The real Gaelic name for the remarkable sea cave on the uninhabited Hebridean island of Staffa is *An Uamh Bhin*, 'the Singing Cave', presumably after the echoic sound made by the tides. But the Ossian poems persuaded Sir Joseph Banks to rename it Fingal's Cave. The romantic composer, Felix Mendelssohn, visited this haunting place, with its perpendicular basalt columns, and wrote an overture, *The Hebrides*, based on the echoes.

FINGAL'S CAVE

PANEL 84 *The Scotsman*, Founded 1817

Panel stitched by:

The Penicuik Team

Joan Cape
Mary Darling
Deborah Hall
Fiona Hutcheson
Isobel Ritchie
Jan Young

Stitched in:
West Linton, Penicuik, Roslin

The Scotsman newspaper, founded as a weekly by a lawyer, William Ritchie, and a customs official, Charles Maclaren, was based in Edinburgh. Apparently a reaction to 'the unblushing subservience' of other papers to the Edinburgh establishment, its motto was 'impartiality, firmness and independence'. It quickly grew popular in the east of Scotland as the newspaper that would become *The Herald*, founded in 1783, dominated in Glasgow and the west. When newspaper stamp tax was abolished in 1850, *The Scotsman* moved to a daily circulation. It has a distinguished history under several notable editors such as Alastair Dunnett, Eric MacKay and Magnus Linklater. *The Scotsman*'s coverage of the arts and the Edinburgh Festival and Fringe in particular has been crucial in the development of Scotland's culture. When Allen Wright, the arts editor, instituted the Fringe Firsts Awards for original drama on the Fringe in 1973, it single-handedly stimulated new work in Britain. More recently, the newspaper has come under pressure as, in line with the sector, its circulation has fallen and valued staff have been laid off. Nevertheless, *The Scotsman* was named Newspaper of the Year in Scotland for 2012.

THE SCOTSMAN FOUNDED 1817

PANEL 85 George Smith and the Glenlivet

Panel stitched by:

Granite Quoins

Zuzana Banicova
Pamela Brice
Pamela Cook
Bruce Duncan
Josephine Duncan
Dilly Emslie
Coral Goldfarb
Heather Hutton
Ewan Jeffrey
Oma Kapilla
Rudra Kapilla
Carole Keepax
Maria Mirick
Michelle Morgan
Tracy Nelson
Sarah Richardson
Catherine Stollery

Stitched in:
Aberdeen, Edinburgh,
Monymusk, Laurencekirk

Whisky production in Scotland was mostly illicit until the early 19th century, made by those anxious to avoid paying excise duty. When George Smith founded the Glenlivet Distillery in 1824, it was unusual for being entirely legal. This made Smith unpopular and he was in the habit of never travelling without a pair of pistols in his belt. He had also to protect his brand from imitators. As it does now, Glenlivet had an excellent reputation. Malt whisky may be said to be one of the few Scottish products that combines the best of Highland and Lowland. Near the distillery at Ballindalloch, Josie's Well supplies pure water from the foothills of the Grampian massif while the barley malt comes from Portgordon in Banffshire. When George Smith died in 1871, his famous brand was being appropriated by others who attached Glenlivet to their own names. Legal action was not entirely successful. Others were permitted to hyphenate Glenlivet but only the product distilled by the Smiths could be called *The* Glenlivet. It has phenomenal sales, being the most popular in the USA and the second best-selling worldwide. Global sales currently run at 6 million bottles. It is to be hoped that Josie's Well never runs dry.

GEORGE SMITH FOUNDS THE GLENLIVET DISTILLERY 1824

PANEL 86 Borders Tweed

Panel stitched by:

Melrose Group

Elizabeth Chalmers
Ruth Dall
Mary Wilson

Stitched in:
Melrose, St Boswells

Walter Scott and his friend, James Hogg, both had a writer's eye for telling detail. Both men and their characters sometimes wore a cloth called the Shepherd's Check or the Shepherd's Plaid. Border weavers had worked the undyed whites, blacks and browns of yarn into the warp and weft to create a rectilinear pattern. Portraits of Scott and Hogg exist of them draped with the check or plaid and it became fashionable. After the visit of George IV in 1822, the manufacture of tartan saw the mills in the Borders become very busy but what really promoted the manufacture of tweed was the wearing of trousers. Until the early 19th century, most men rode horses and wore breeches. But, in 1829, a diarist, Archibald Craig, recorded men wearing trousers made from Shepherd's check with a black coat. Colours were introduced and, in 1830, a London tailor, an expatriate Scot called James Locke, visited Galashiels to encourage the mill owners to create pattern books of tweed and tartan so that he could show it to customers. Reluctantly, they agreed. At the same time, suits were becoming fashionable – jackets and trousers made from the same cloth and pattern. Locke coined a new name for the output of the Border mills when he sold it as tweed and tweed suits became the acme of good taste. The rest is sartorial history.

PANEL 87 The Growth of Glasgow

Panel stitched by:

Glasgow Society of Women Artists

Helen Abdy
Susan Black
Lyn Dunachie
Adrianne Foulds
Netta Hunter
Margaret Murphy
Ingrid Parker
Ann Rennie
Ann Wilson

Stitched in:
Glasgow

By the 1820s, Glasgow's population had outgrown Edinburgh's. The Tobacco Lords had had a deep water port dredged as far upriver as Port Glasgow but, into the 19th century, the volume of trade persuaded investment in allowing merchant ships to dock in the heart of the city. In 1795, the Forth-Clyde Canal opened with its terminus at Port Dundas and this brought the raw materials of Lanarkshire into the city. Glasgow was growing very fast and became one of the earliest European cities to reach a population of one million. By the end of the 19th century, it was known as 'The Second City of the Empire' and the city's motto, 'Let Glasgow Flourish', was never more apposite. Shipbuilding and heavy engineering clustered close to the river but, across the city, textile and carpet manufacture, cigarette making, printing and publishing and all manner of industry were providing employment and making fortunes. The 19th century saw the building of the Kelvingrove Art Gallery, the Mitchell Library and the City Chambers. There was a palpable sense of civic pride and one of its exemplars was William Burrell. A ruthless ship owner who had the nerve to buy at the bottom of the market and sell at the top, he was also a near-obsessive art collector. After his death in 1958, he bequeathed his fabulous collection to Glasgow and the building that houses it in Pollok Park is a shared delight.

DESTITUTION · AGITATION · REPRESSION · PROCLAMATION · TRANSPORTATION · EXECUTION · INDUSTRIALISATION · IMMIGRATION · INNOVATION · EXPANSION

COTTON ⊙ BREWING ⊙ WEAVING ⊙

RIVER CLYDE

LET GLASGOW FLOURISH

THE GROWTH OF GLASGOW c1820s

PANEL 88 Sheep Shearing

Panel stitched by:

Pentland Stitches

Ali Cameron
Sara-Jayne Donaldson
Hilda Ibrahim
Angela E Lewis
Meg Macleod
Ann Mair
Carmel Ross

Stitched in:
Thurso, Dunnet, Caithness

Wool was pulled or combed out of fleeces before sheep were sheared and as the animals shed winter wool, this could be relatively easy. But, as wool production intensified in the Middle Ages, fleeces had to be sheared in the spring clip, often before lambing if the weather was not too cold. Washing the wool was a significant part of the process and there is a Scots song that remembers oily or tarry *oo*, the word for wool:

Tarry Oo, Tarry Oo,
Tarry Oo is ill tae spin,
Caird it weel, caird it weel,
Caird it weel ere ye begin.
When 'tis cairded, row'd and spun,
Then the wark is halflins done,
But when woven, drest and clean,
It may be cleading for a queen.

HI

PENTLAND STITCHES

PANEL 89 The First Reform Act

Panel stitched by:

Pentland Stitchers

Tish Alderson
Anne Chater
Lois-May Donaldson
Aileen Gardiner
Diana Gordon Smith
Viv Henderson
Anthea Johnston
Jeannie Laidlaw
Caroline Pearson
Mary Warrack

Stitched in:
Edinburgh, Milnathort,
Eskbank, Dalkeith

In the brief reign of William IV, this long overdue piece of legislation redistributed parliamentary seats to reflect the great changes wrought by the Industrial Revolution. Separate acts were passed for Scotland, Ireland, and England and Wales but the effects were similar. Rotten boroughs such as Grampound in Cornwall or Dunwich in Suffolk elected two MPs even though only a handful of men had the vote in each village. Steered through parliament by Earl Grey (also famous for tea), the acts ensured new constituencies were created for burgeoning cities such as Manchester and Glasgow. Counties could elect two members, known as Knights of the Shires, and universities retained representation in the House of Commons. Until 1918, Edinburgh and St Andrews, in a unique cooperation, elected a joint MP, as did Glasgow and Aberdeen. In 1832, the electorate was all male and consisted only of a tiny proportion of the population at around 500,000. Voters were property owners whose land or houses was reckoned to be worth a certain sum and those who owned two or more houses in different constituencies were allowed to vote more than once. The Reform Act increased the franchise to 813,000. In Scotland, the rise was much more dramatic. Before the Act, only 4,239 could vote and this increased to more than 65,000. Aberdeen, Dundee and Perth were awarded MPs for the first time.

JOHN KING AGNES MOFFAT

FIRST REPORT COMMISSIONERS OF MINES 1842

FIRST REFORM ACT 1832

PANEL 90 Kirkpatrick Macmillan

Panel stitched by:

Pans People

Susan Findlay
Frances Glynn
Avril Harris

Stitched in:
Prestonpans, Longniddry

A blacksmith born in 1812 at Keir in Dumfries and Galloway, Kirkpatrick Macmillan invented the machine that his countryman, Sir Chris Hoy, cycled to Olympic glory. A plaque on the smiddy wall at Courthill records that '[h]e builded better than he knew'. In 1839, Macmillan made a wooden prototype with iron-rimmed wheels, something a blacksmith will have been skilled at, and a steerable front wheel. But crucially the back wheel could be powered by pedals connected to it by rigid rods, following the principles laid down by James Watt. Macmillan's relative, James Johnston, set out in the 1890s 'to prove that to my native country of Dumfries belongs the honour of being the birthplace of the invention of the bicycle'. Such an upfront statement invites scepticism but this should all be ignored. Like James Small, Kirkpartick Macmillan was clearly a talented inventor, one of a long line of Scots who added to the enjoyment and convenience of all. And how else can Sir Chris Hoy's phenomenal, natural, intuitive talent be explained? Bicycles are part of Scotland's heritage, then and now.

THE BICYCLE

VULCAN FOUNDRY

THOMAS McCALL KILMARNOCK

MY NAME COUNTY OF DUMFRIES BELONGS THE HONOUR OF BEING THE BIRTHPLACE OF THE INVENTION OF

KEIR MILL DUMFRIES

KIRKPATRICK MACMILLAN

HE BUILDED BETTER THAN HE KNEW

PANEL 91 Queen Victoria at Balmoral

Panel stitched by:

Glenisla

Heather Berger
Claire Broadhurst
Sheila Bruce
Catriona Campbell
Pippa Clegg
Olive Duncan
Jeanette McGill
Mary Ogilvie
Christine Palmer
Kirsty Palmer

Stitched in:
Blairgowrie, Abernyte,
Edinburgh, Kirriemuir

Queen Victoria and Prince Albert fell in love with Scotland. After their first visit in 1842, they came back often, particularly to the Highlands. Preferring the slightly less rainy climate of Deeside, Albert eventually bought the Balmoral Estate and spent much of his summers shooting deer and other game. Where royalty led, the gentry followed and many imitations of Balmoral were built – so-called shooting lodges sprang up on many lochsides, some of them vast piles that lay empty for most of the year. Highland balls were a royal favourite and, once again, the court set the pace for the British aristocracy as they reeled, strathspeyed and sweated around dance floors in kilts, plaids and thick woollen hose. Tartan and all things Highland became fashionable. Balmorality was born and, with the annual holiday of the royal family, it continues. Bafflingly Queen Victoria announced that, at heart, she was a Jacobite. Her diary extracts from 1848 to 1861, *Leaves from the Journal of Our Life in the Highlands*, was a best-seller and, in the railway age, it brought many tourists north. Just as they were arriving, many Highlanders were leaving, some of them cleared off their land by force.

VICTORIA AT BALMORAL 1850s/60s

DASH

GLENISLA GROUP

PANEL 92 The Scots in India

Panel stitched by:

Wardie Church Stitchers

Ann Bell
Karen Bowman
Susan Dyer
Rhona Else
Susan Fraser
Jean Jenkins
Frances Mackinnon
Fiona Mauritzen
Jane Prowse
Barbara Purdie
Janet Rust
Susie Standley
Jean Temple

Stitched in:
Edinburgh

After the victories of the Seven Years War and the prowess of Robert Clive and the armies of the East India Company, India became a vast source of raw materials for British industry as well as a market for manufactured goods. Until the middle of the 19th century, the subcontinent was controlled by this private company. It could conclude treaties, fight wars and defy governments. Henry Dundas was appointed President of the Board of Control and he oversaw the recruitment of many Scots in India. By 1792, one in nine working for the Company was Scots and a third of all the officers in its armies. Many fortunes were made. Scots invested so heavily in the India tea trade that production outstripped that of China. Dundee became a centre for the processing of jute. A vegetable fibre, it was used for making sacking, carpet and linoleum backing and many other purposes. So many Scots were resident in Calcutta, now Kolkata, that a regiment known as the Calcutta Scots was raised for the Indian army.

SCOTS IN INDIA

PANEL 93   The Disruption

Panel stitched by:

Heirs of 1843

Fiona Anderson
Marie Austin
Winifred Cumming
Lilias Finlay
Mary Godden
Nan Laird
Dorothy MacKenzie
Jean Mackinlay
Christine MacPhail
Deborah Miller
Elizabeth Mitchell
Maggie Morley
Jean Morrison
Judith Pickles
Maggie Romanis

Stitched in:
Edinburgh

By 1843, tensions within the Church of Scotland had reached breaking point. The central issue concerned who had the right to appoint a minister to a parish – the laird or the kirk session. It struck chords with a bloody past, when battles had been fought over the related issue of independence for the kirk. Led by Thomas Chalmers, the Evangelical Party opposed the right (enshrined in an act of 1712) of lairds to 'prefer' their candidates while the Moderates supported it – because it was the law. At the General Assembly of the Church of Scotland, held in St Andrew and St George's in Edinburgh, a staged walkout took place. The retiring Moderator, Dr David Welsh, led 121 ministers and 73 elders out of the established church and down to Tanfield Hall in Canonmills. There they constituted themselves as The Free Church of Scotland. Eventually 474 ministers out of about 1,200 came out. It was an act of real bravery. Most lost their manses and kirks immediately since they were the property of the Church of Scotland and a frantic building programme began that almost doubled the number of churches, church halls and manses in Scotland. By a quirk of history, the Disruption inadvertently created the circumstances in Edinburgh where the Festival Fringe could find performance spaces and flourish. The Disruption was also the first great public event to be recorded by photography. After parliament rescinded the act of 1712 in 1929, the kirk was reunited, almost.

PANEL 94
David Octavius Hill and Robert Adamson

Panel stitched by:

Floral Ring

Annalise McBride
Margot Miller
Hazel Stewart
Heather Young

Stitched in:
Edinburgh

A painter, Hill, joined Adamson, an engineer, to create the first photographic studio in Scotland. It was based at Rock House at the western end of Calton Hill in Edinburgh. Most of the early photographs, known as calotypes, were portraits, many of them shot out of doors. Not only did they provide a record of the Disruption, the two also began to photograph outdoor scenes, landscapes and working people. They particularly enjoyed shooting the work of the fishermen of Newhaven and the fishwives who walked up to Edinburgh to sell the fresh catch round the doors. Even though the studio and the partnership only lasted five years, the output was prodigious, the earliest photographic record of life in Scotland.

PANEL 95 The Railway Boom

Panel stitched by:

Fifan Leddies

Margaret Caldwell
Jennifer di Folco
Margaret Ewan

Stitched in:
Burntisland, Anstruther

Railways were built in Scotland from the 1830s onwards but, for some time, there was no network. The earliest were industrial, transporting coal and other raw materials between Glasgow, Dundee and Edinburgh. But, by 1842, investment was pouring in as the Edinburgh to Glasgow line opened and the Caledonian Company linked with the English rail network at Carlisle in 1848. Its great rival was the North British Railway and, in order to challenge and dominate the lines in the east of Scotland, it had to build bridges. The first spanned the Firth of Tay and opened in 1878 only to collapse a year later in a storm with the loss of 75 lives. The Forth Bridge was deliberately designed to look much stronger and it is the first structure in the world to be built of steel. Opened in 1890, its elegant cantilever construction has become an icon and, in any competition to decide the most famous manmade structure in Scotland, the Forth Bridge would surely win. Its completion opened up the north of Scotland to rapid rail travel. Contrary to popular belief, the bridge does not need constant repainting. A contract was completed in 2011 that should ensure that no repainting is needed until 2046 at the earliest.

EIGHTH WONDER OF THE WORLD

THERE'S A LINE OF SYMMETRY TO CATCH THE WATCHER'S EYE

DESIGNERS ENGINEERS • THE BRIGGERS CONTRACTOR • DRILLERS DIVERS • CAISSON WORKERS ROPEMAKERS • BOILERMAKERS STONEMASONS • MACHINE MEN TINSMITHS • RIVETERS CATCHERS • JOINERS PAINTERS • INSPECTORS LABOURERS • ENGINE DRIVERS AMBULANCE MEN

FIFANLEDDIES

THE RAILWAY BOOM AND THE FORTH RAIL BRIDGE

PANEL 96 The Caithness School, 1851

Panel stitched by:

Caithness Textile Artists

Valerie Barker
Joan Dancer
Louise Hunt
Dorothy Johnston
Ella Lawrence
Shirley MacLeod
Celia More
Catherine Swanson

Stitched in:
Lybster, Wick, Thurso,
Halkirk

By the 19th century, the dream of John Knox and the reformers had been realised. There was a school in almost every parish in Scotland and one of the consequences was a high level of mass literacy. At between 70 and 77 per cent, it was highest in Britain in the counties of Caithness and Berwickshire. But the picture was patchy. In Lanarkshire, attendance at school was below 50 per cent. But, when school boards came into existence in 1872 and they took over much of education from the church, standards rose. Scotland's universities, especially Glasgow, pioneered the needs of students drawn from an urban and middle-class background rather than simply providing an education for the gentry. It offered degrees in law, medicine, engineering, science, and divinity. Entrance qualifications were standardised and women were admitted in the 1890s, with St Andrews taking the lead. Education continues to be set at a premium in Scotland – at least in theory. But the brief window that allowed children to progress from school to university with fees paid by the local authority and a maintenance grant from the Scottish Education Department is now closed. This obviously restricts the number of talented young people who can benefit from Scotland's great educational tradition.

A CAITHNESS SCHOOL 1851

PANEL 97 Fitba

Panel stitched by:

The Glasgow Banner Group

Marilyn Caddell
Clare Hunter
Mary McCarron
Grace Pratt
Norma Ventisei
Agnes Wylie

Stitched in:
Bishopbriggs, Uddington,
Balquhidder, Lanark

Futeball is recorded as early as 1424, when it was outlawed. But what might seem like football now was played all over Scotland. Ancient versions, like the Jethart Hand Ba' game, do not involve much kicking – of the ball, at least – but other variants do. It was not until the 1860s and 1870s that football's laws were codified and the first association of clubs was in England. Queens Park in Glasgow was founded in 1867 and it played against English opposition, reaching the FA Cup final twice. The first international match between Scotland and England took place in 1872. It was a 0–0 draw but the first time the Scottish football team played in navy blue jerseys with a thistle embroidered on the breast was two years later. They borrowed the design from the national rugby team. Scottish clubs began to form, mainly in the west at first, and the second oldest cup competition in the world began in 1873 with the Scottish Cup. Vale of Leven and Queens Park dominated the early years. Players were paid almost from the outset and Scotland's largest and wealthiest clubs have traditionally been Rangers and Celtic (although Rangers have recently fallen on hard times) and the first Old Firm match was played on Glasgow Green. After the Second World War, Scottish football enjoyed some glorious episodes. In 1967, Celtic became the first British side to win the European Cup and, in 1972, Rangers won the Cup Winners' Cup. But, since the mid 1970s, there has been a general decline – apart from Alex Ferguson's achievements at Aberdeen in the early 1980s – and the national side has fallen far down the world rankings. But hope springs eternal.

PANEL 98 Irish Immigration after the Famine

Panel stitched by:

Trinity Stitchers

Joyce Ager
Muriel Cleland
Doreen Guy

Stitched in:
Edinburgh, North Berwick

During the devastating potato blight in Ireland and the famine that followed between 1845 to 1851, emigration to Scotland accelerated rapidly. At its peak in 1848, the average number of immigrants disembarking weekly at the quays in Glasgow was estimated at more than a thousand and between January and April of that year, 42,860 came. Even in a city expanding as fast as Victorian Glasgow, this influx was dramatic – probably the most intense episode of immigration into Scotland for a thousand years. Many quickly found jobs in the heavy industries clustering around the coalfields of North Lanarkshire. It was hard, menial and frustrating work. Many Irish Catholics found it difficult to rise through the ranks of skilled workers but, after the horrors of the Great Famine, these jobs put bread on the table and roofs over the heads of families. Founded in 1887 by the Irish Marist Brother Walfrid, Celtic Football Club had a social as well as a sporting purpose and the club soon began to prosper. In 1888, the first Old Firm match with Rangers took place. Celtic won 5–2 but many of their players had been signed from Hibernian Football Club in Edinburgh. The two clubs became emblematic of the tensions between Catholics and Protestants in Scotland but mercifully most of the violence is now usually confined to the football pitch.

IRISH IMMIGRATION AFTER THE FAMINE
FOUNDING OF CELTIC AND RANGERS FOOTBALL CLUBS

PANEL 99 James Clerk Maxwell

Panel stitched by:

The Gladsmuir Group

Patricia Coupe
Pru Irvine
Susanne Lowe
Celia Williams

Stitched in:
Gladsmuir, West Garleton,
Pencaitland, Pathhead

Born in Edinburgh in 1831, this brilliant but sometimes underestimated scientist brought a series of equations, experiments and observations about electricity, optics and magnetism together into a consistent theory. He argued convincingly that all three phenomena are manifestations of the electromagnetic field. In 1865, Maxwell showed that electrical and magnetic fields move through space as waves that travel at the speed of light. At the age of only 25, he was appointed Professor of Natural Philos-ophy at Aberdeen University. The Adams Prize, given by St John's College, Cambridge, chose as its topic the apparent stability of the rings around Saturn. Maxwell postulated that they were composed of small particles, each of which independently orbited the planet. Not only did he win the prize but, in 1980, the Voyager space exploration programme proved him right. Interested in optics and the study of colour vision, Maxwell's research made colour photography possible. Despite his pioneering work across many fields of science, James Clerk Maxwell seems not to have taken himself too seriously. Based on the song 'Comin' Through the Rye' by Robert Burns, he composed his own version to reflect his interest in physics:

> Gin a body meet a body
> Flyin' through the air.
> Gin a body hit a body,
> Will it fly? And where?

Maxwell sadly died young of cancer at the age of 48 but his contribution to modern scientific thought was immense.

PANEL 100 Scots in Africa

Panel stitched by:

St Blanes Group

Judith Abbott
Caroline B. Buchanan
Maud Crawford
Sarah Gammell
Fiona Gibson
Jenny Haldane
Dorothy Morton
Libby Taylor
Anne Thomson

Stitched in:
Auchterarder,
Cambusbarron, Dunblane,
Murthly, Callander,
Port of Menteith, Duns

Despite their involvement with the infamous slave trade, Scots made a positive contribution to the story of Africa in the 19th and early 20th centuries. Perhaps the most famous was David Livingstone, a medical missionary and explorer who sought to discover the sources of the River Nile. His meeting on 10 November 1871, with H. M. Stanley is immortalised in the quote, 'Dr Livingstone, I presume?' Since the explorer's own account does not mention this amusing piece of irony and Stanley later tore out the relevant pages of his journal, the phrase may be a fabrication. But it is a good line anyway. Mary Slessor was a missionary who penetrated deep into the Calabar region of West Africa. It was difficult for a woman but, in some ways, her gender made her less threatening. She preached against witchcraft, human sacrifice and the abandonment of twins. Slessor died of malaria in 1915. Alexander Gordon Laing was the first European to reach the fabled city of Timbuktu. On an expedition across the Sahara Desert, from north to south, in 1826 and despite being wounded in Tuareg attacks, he entered the city. But the intrepid Laing was murdered soon afterwards and his valuable papers lost. Tragedy was mixed with Scottish dourness. Mungo Park discovered the middle reaches of the great River Niger. He was born on the farm of Foulshiels, near Selkirk, in 1771 and, when he came back home in 1793 after many years abroad, his mother and brothers heard a knock at the door. 'Aye,' said one of his brothers, 'that'll be Mungo.' 'How do you know?' asked his mother. 'I saw him get off the coach in Selkirk.' was the reply. No matter how renowned, no one gets above themselves in Scotland.

CALABAR

MARY SLESSOR

VICTORIA FALLS

MUNGO PARK

THE NIGER

DAVID LIVINGSTONE

HUGH CLAPPERTON

ALEXANDER GORDON LAING

TIMBUKTU

SCOTLAND IN AFRICA

PANEL 101 Highland Games

Panel stitched by:

Strathpeffer Craft &
Craic Group

Carole Bancroft
Mary Bethune
Janet Bowen
Kit Bowen
Patricia Haigh
Clara Hickey
Morag Hickey
Pat Justad
Laura Lee McWhinney
Alison Munro-White
Audrey North
Denise Page
Grace Ritchie

Stitched in:
Strathpeffer, Garve

These tartan-clad summer celebrations of caber tossing, Highland dancing, bagpiping, heavy and light events and general conviviality are mostly a Victorian invention – a cheery facet of Balmorality. But some of the events or individual sporting contests are clearly much older. Perhaps the most idiosyncratic is *Maide Leisg*, Gaelic for 'Lazy Stick'. It involves two men sitting on the ground with the soles of their feet pressed against each other. Between them, they hold a stick in their hands and attempt to pull each other up until one is raised off the ground. It is generally believed to be the oldest event at the Carloway Highland Games on the Isle of Lewis. There are 14 major Highland Games held each year in Scotland, most of them north of the Highland Line. In the USA there are 147 and one in Switzerland. The greatest athlete ever to compete in the heavy events was probably Bill Anderson. He won 16 Scottish Championship titles from 1959 to 1974 and was American champion from 1976 to 1980. The Scots Hammer, wooden shafted and thrown from a standing position, was Anderson's most successful event and his world record of 123 feet, 5 inches still stands unbeaten.

PANEL 102 Scottish Rugby

Panel stitched by:

The Mascots

Margaret Ferguson Burns
Maeve Greer
Kathleen Grigor
Margaret Hill
Janet Speirs

Stitched in:
Edinburgh

The Scottish Rugby Union was at first a Glasgow and Edinburgh affair with all the founding clubs except one coming from the cities. And, even though the game's heartland was in the Borders, it continued to be run by clubs of former pupils of Edinburgh and Glasgow schools for many years. Selection for international matches could be idiosyncratic and, until the era of league rugby in the early 1980s, Borders players had to have irresistible talent to be selected. The first match between England and Scotland was played in 1871 at Raeburn Place in Edinburgh and the Scots triumphed by a try to nil. It has been downhill ever since. Nevertheless, the amateur era was attractive, even romantic. Players could be heroes at Murrayfield on an international Saturday but they returned to their work on Monday as though very little had happened. One gnarled Borders prop forward scored a try against France in Paris but, as he cycled to his work as a railwayman on the Monday morning, he was accosted in the street by two old ladies who demanded to know why his wits had deserted him – why had he not run behind the French posts to make the conversion easier? In the days of the amateur game, Scotland could occasionally field a team to beat the best (except New Zealand), with victories over England being especially sweet. However, now that players are paid, Scotland rarely punches above its demographic weight. But, as with football, there is hope – especially at the beginning of each new season. Maybe this time . . .

SCOTTISH RUGBY UNION FOUNDED 1873,
FIRST MATCH BETWEEN ENGLAND AND SCOTLAND 1871

PANEL 103 Shinty and Curling

Panel stitched by:

Susie Finlayson
Linda Jobson

Stitched in:
Eskbank, Dalkeith

In addition to golf and, arguably, rugby, Scotland has given two other distinctive games to the world. Shinty is a robust form of hockey, with its most recognisable descendant probably being ice hockey. Unlike the genteel English version, shinty involves shoulder-charge tackling, tackling with the stick or caman, playing the ball in the air (the source of a few head injuries) and other moves only occasionally recognised in the rule book. Now it is played mostly in the Highlands where famous teams like Kingussie, Newtonmore and Fort William have dominated. In the 19th and early 20th centuries, the game was popular in England, especially in Lancashire and Nottinghamshire. Some modern players have suggested that, for her Harry Potter books, J. K. Rowling was inspired by shinty to invent quidditch. Curling is more international and the game is firmly established in Canada, the USA, Switzerland, Sweden and elsewhere. It is also an Olympic sport. With immense precision, curling stones are slid down a long rectangular rink of ice to settle in a circular target zone or to knock a rival's stone out of contention. Made from granite, much of it quarried from Ailsa Craig in the Firth of Clyde, the stones make a noise when sliding down the rink. This has given rise to the phrase 'the roaring game'. In a hard Scottish winter, when lochs and rivers freeze, many very occasional curlers dust off ancient stones and take to the ice and they often roar.

Scots in North America

Panel stitched by:

Sally Wild
Frances Fettes

Stitched in:
Eskbank

In the decades immediately following the American Revolutionary War of 1775–1783, Scots, seen as loyalists, were unpopular. But into the 19th century, as emigration accelerated, several expatriate Scotsmen played leading roles in shaping the USA. Born in Dunfermline in 1835, the son of a weaver, Andrew Carnegie emigrated with his father and family in 1848. Fanatically hard-working and self-improving (through the use of libraries), the young Carnegie rose quickly through the ranks of the Pennsylvania Railroad Company. He began to borrow money to invest in railway-related companies and, after the American Civil War (1861–65), made huge profits. In 1901, he formed US Steel and it was the first company to be worth more than a billion dollars. Carnegie's philanthropy was also immense and perhaps his greatest legacy is the network of libraries he funded in Scotland. John Muir was very different. A naturalist and an advocate for the active preservation of the natural world, he helped set up the Yosemite and Sequoia national parks. The Sierra Club, which he founded, is one of the most important conservation organisations in the USA. According to his biographer, Donald Worster, Muir's mission was 'saving the American soul from total surrender to materialism'. Known as *Aglooka*, 'Long Strider', by the Inuit, John Rae explored Northern Canada in the mid 19th century. Originally from Orkney, he understood that the best way to survive Arctic conditions was to imitate the indigenous peoples in their clothing and way of life. Canada's northern regions were mapped by Rae and his work was consolidated by Sandford Fleming, a Scottish-born surveyor and map maker. He also designed the first Canadian postage stamp and proposed a system of worldwide standard time. After missing a train in Ireland, he produced a plan for a series of time zones based on the Greenwich meridian and, by 1919, it had been adopted. Scots pioneered much in and beyond North America.

SCOTS IN AMERICA 19TH CENTURY EMIGRATION

PANEL 105 The Paisley Pattern

Panel stitched by:

C plus 3

Lorna Chapman
Catherine Hughes
Julie MacNaughton
Hazel Pert

Stitched in:
Glasgow

In the late 18th century, soldiers returning from the wars in India brought back silk and woollen Kashmir shawls decorated with the *boteh*, a droplet-shaped vegetable motif of Persian or Indian origin. From c. 1800 onwards, weavers in Paisley began to produce shawls with this design. Their looms were sufficiently sophisticated to allow them to weave with five colours of yarn. The *boteh* quickly became known as the Paisley pattern and, in the 19th century, it was printed on cotton and woollen shawls and headsquares. Printed Paisley pattern was much cheaper than woven and almost as fashionable.

THE MILL'S GAEN FAST

PANEL 106 The Battle of the Braes

Panel stitched by:

Skye Quilt Studio

Sue Cooper
Irene Curren
Lin Leighton
Jennifer Lewis
Liz Macleod
Ann Nicolson
Irene Owen
Barbara Rutterford
Anne Trimmer
Shirley Urquhart

Stitched in:
Skye

In 1882, after more than a century of oppression following the defeat at Culloden, crofting communities on Skye refused to accept it anymore and violence flared. When tenants were faced with eviction from farmland in the Braes district south of Portree, they withheld payment of rent and also herded their sheep to graze on the slopes of Ben Lee, an area expressly forbidden to them. It had formerly been common land but it was seized by Lord Macdonald's men after the Clearances. When a Sheriff Officer arrived from Portree to serve the eviction notices, an angry mob burned them in front of him. Women were especially active and vocal. Fifty policemen were summoned from Glasgow to enforce Lord Macdonald's will but, after they arrested the men responsible for burning the notices of eviction, they were attacked by a large mob. Three hundred men and women fought in the Battle of the Braes and seven women were badly injured by truncheon blows. Prisoners were tried and convicted without a jury. Newspapers expressed outrage and MPs called for an inquiry. Unrest spread to Glendale where more violence erupted. Astonishingly, a negotiator was sent to Skye, on board a navy gunboat, and it was agreed that, if the Glendale men stood trial, a Royal commission would be set up. Known as the Napier Commission, it proposed mild reforms but, after four crofter MPs were elected in 1885, the Crofters' Act was passed. Much more radical, it gave every crofter security of tenure. Immune from eviction, they were now able to pass on their crofts to their heirs. It was a remarkable and long overdue victory.

BATTLE OF THE BRAES, SKYE, 1882, NAPIER COMMISSION

PANEL 107 Mill Working

Panel stitched by:

Frances Gardiner
Gillian Hart
Yvonne Murphy
Jeannie Roberts
Dorie Wilkie

Stitched in:
Port Seton, North Berwick

As Paisley Pattern and other distinctive designs grew more popular, spinning and weaving were increasingly industrialised in Scotland. The outworkers who drove the looms and knitting frames at home, often with their wives and family carding and spinning yarn, were usually men. But as demand grew and entrepreneurs invested in scale, weavers and spinners moved into mills. At first water-driven and then steam-powered, with the coming of the railways, the mills also took on more and more women. The larger mechanical looms often needed delicate fingers to tease out problems and the muscle-power that drove the foot pedals of the domestic frames and looms became less important. Many of the beautiful shawls and fabric woven in Paisley and the west of Scotland were exported through Glasgow.

Robert Louis Stevenson

Panel stitched by:

Stitchers wi' Smeddum

Ann Dickson
Lynn Fraser
Janet Macaulay
Liz Neilson

Stitched in:
Tranent, Pencaitland

Few writers have written masterpiece after masterpiece but *Treasure Island*, *Kidnapped*, *The Strange Case of Dr Jekyll and Mr Hyde* and *The Master of Ballantrae* have left an indelible mark. And, for TV watchers and filmgoers of a certain age, *The Black Arrow*, *The Wrong Box* and *St Ives* were an early and thrilling introduction to the work of Robert Louis Stevenson. Unfussy in his language, brilliant in plot structure and characterisation, he was a genius, an original, a truly great writer. And yet the *Oxford Anthology of English Literature* managed no mention of him or his work in more than 2,000 pages and, for decades of the 20th century, so-called critics consigned Stevenson to the ghetto of children's literature. Born in Edinburgh, he began writing when very young but, by the age of 23, his health began to become a problem. Stevenson spent much of his short life looking for a climate in which he might thrive. Between 1880 and 1887, his most famous books were published. By 1888, the famous author was in the Pacific and, in 1890, he bought land in Samoa. There he took the name of *Tusitala*, 'the Teller of Tales'. In 1894, Stevenson collapsed and died, only 44 years old. Here is the well-known and much misquoted epitaph he wrote for himself:

> Under the wide and starry sky
> Dig the grave and let me lie.
> Glad did I live and gladly die,
> And I laid me down with a will.
>
> This be the verse you grave for me:
> Here he lies where he longed to be;
> Home is the sailor, home from sea,
> And the hunter home from the hill.

Fiction is to grown men
What play is to the child.
RLS

Black

The Land of Counterpane
When I was sick and lay abed,
I had two pillows at my head,
And all my toys beside me lay,
To keep me happy all the day.

FIDRA

TUSITALA TELLER OF TALES

DREAMER OF DREAMS ON GOSSAMER SAILS

SWANSTON

ROBERT LOUIS STEVENSON

Workshop of the Empire

Panel stitched by:

Linlithgow Stitchers

Christine Anderson
Hazel Briton
Gloria Fleming
Aileen Rasberry
Valerie Spence
Patricia Swan

Stitched in:
Linlithgow, Falkirk

The Lanarkshire coalfield and the deposits of iron ore that lay nearby combined with Glasgow's status as a busy Atlantic port to spark the city's great industrial development. Once it became possible to transport these raw materials in bulk by canal and then by rail, shipbuilding, railway locomotive and carriage building and other heavy engineering flourished. And what these industries produced could be readily exported through the Glasgow quays. Parkhead Forge may now be a shopping centre but in the 19th and early 20th centuries it was the largest steelworks in Scotland, employing more than 20,000 men at its height. Four railway manufacturers had plants in the Springburn District. St Rollox grew to be the largest and it is still operational as a rolling stock repair and maintenance facility. Heavy industry may have predominated in the 19th century in the west of Scotland where its output found ready markets in the developing infrastructure of the colonies of the Empire but other sorts of manufacturing were also important. Textiles, especially the spinning and weaving of cotton, flourished until the American Civil War cut off supplies in the 1860s. Coal mining powered much of Scotland's industry until the second half of the 20th century but by that time heavy engineering was declining. And the gradual disappearance of the vast market that was the British Empire was a fundamental reason for the shrinkage of Scottish manufacturing, one of its workshops.

The Scottish Trades Union Congress Forms

Panel stitched by:

Clydeside 5

Rosalind Jarvis
Jane Logan
Jacky Mackenzie
Jim Mulrine
Carol Woodward

Stitched in:
Glasgow

Representing 630,000 members of 39 affiliated trades unions, the STUC is separate from the TUC, the British Trades Union Congress. In the voting for the first Parliamentary Committee 1897 (later the General Council), Miss M. H. Irwin gained the most support but, on the grounds that such a thing was politically premature, she declined to be chairman. Margaret Irwin was raised in St Andrews and took an early form of degree from the university. Involved with the Women's Suffrage movement, she was secretary of the Scottish Council for Women's Trades and central to the setting up of the STUC. The first woman to occupy the role of chairman was Miss Bell Jobson in 1937. The STUC was seen as more radical than the English TUC with many of its leaders being members of the Independent Labour Party. Its goal was 'to secure the collective ownership of the means of production, distribution and exchange' – a dictum only recently removed from the philosophy of the modern Labour Party.

UNITY IS STRENGTH

FELLOWSHIP IS LIFE

MARGARET IRWIN

March 25th

ROBERT SMILLIE

KELVIN

HARLAND & WOLF

BARCLAY CURLE

FAIRFIELDS

CONNELL

STEPHENS

RIVER CLYDE

YARROW

BLYTHSWOOD

SHIELDHALL

SIMONS

JOHN BROWNS

CART

CLYDESIDE

5

SCOTTISH TRADES UNION CONGRESS FORMS IN GLASGOW 1897

Keir Hardie

Panel stitched by:

Smith Stitchers

Rita Smith
Shirley Smith
Audrey Smith

Stitched in:
Falkirk, Glasgow

Born in 1856 in a one-room cottage near Holytown in Lanarkshire, Keir Hardie had a meteoric rise. From being a miner, he became a union organiser and was then elected as MP for West Ham South in London in 1892. A year later, he and others formed the Independent Labour Party. After making a speech in parliament attacking the monarchy, Hardie lost his London seat but was later elected MP for Merthyr Tydfil and Aberdare, a constituency he served for the rest of his life. In the 1906 Liberal landslide, Labour won 29 seats and began to grow into a powerful political force. Two years later, Hardie resigned as Labour leader and became closely involved with campaigning for votes for women. Highly principled, he was a pacifist and was appalled by the slaughter of the First World War. He contacted socialist colleagues in other countries in order to organise an international general strike to bring the fighting to an end. Deeply unpopular, Hardie nevertheless persisted and made anti-war speeches wherever and whenever he could. But, a year after the outbreak of hostilities, he suffered a series of strokes and died in hospital in Glasgow on 26 September 1915.

PANEL 112 The Herring Girls

Panel stitched by:

Herring Gulls

Alison Dickson
Janet Raeburn

Stitched in:
North Berwick

Known as *Clann-Nighean an Sgadain*, many of the Herring Girls came from the Hebrides and their seasonal work followed the herring catch around the coasts of Scotland. Particularly from the 1840s onwards, they moved from the ports at Lerwick on Shetland down to Wick, Fraser-burgh, Peterhead, all the way down to Eyemouth and then further south to the quaysides of Yarmouth and Lowestoft. Their job was to gut the herring catch and pack it into barrels where the fish was preserved in brine. Working at tremendous speed, the *Clann-Nighean* worked in crews of three with two gutting and a third, usually the tallest, packing because she could reach the bottom of the barrel more easily. The guts were also saved and used as a noxious fertiliser by farmers. The women worked incredibly quickly and the average number of fish they gutted in a minute was 40 but it could be much higher. Of course, they often sang as they worked.

MONTROSE
ABERDEEN
PITTENWEEM
ANSTRUTHER
CRAIL
STONEHAVEN
LOCHRANZA

MALLAIG
FISHERROW
PORT SETON
ULLAPOOL
PORTREE
STORNOWAY
OBAN
ARBROATH
LERWICK
PETERHEAD
FRASERBURGH
NORTH BERWICK
PORTSOY

WICK
DUNBAR
EYEMOUTH
BERWICK

CULLEN
BUCKIE
LOSSIEMOUTH

FA' WAD BE A FISHER QUINE
GUTTIN HERRIN FRAE THE BRINE?

GREAT YARMOUTH

JR AD

PANEL 113   The *Discovery* Sails from Dundee

Panel stitched by:

Barbara Bell
Ursula Doherty
Tessa Durham
Catherine Jones
Dawn White

Stitched in:
Newport on Tay

Launched in 1901, the *Discovery* was the last traditional wooden, three-masted ship to be built in Britain. Designated RRS, Royal Research Ship, she was designed for the British National Antarctic Expedition led by Ernest Shackleton and Robert Falcon Scott. The hull was built of wood so that it would not be frozen into the ice and the bow was designed in such a way that it would rise up over the pack ice and break it by its deadweight. The expedition sighted the Antarctic coastline on 8 January 1902 and dropped anchor in McMurdo Sound. For the next two years, locked into the ice, the ship would remain there as the crew surveyed and mapped the coastline. The *Discovery* expedition was reckoned a success since its crew were able to show that Antarctica was a continent, they relocated magnetic south and made excellent maps and charts. Using controlled explosives, the ship was freed from the ice in February 1904 and it docked at Spithead seven months later. Despite its success, the British Antarctic Expedition found itself in financial difficulties and the ship was sold to the Hudson's Bay Company. After a long career in various roles, the RRS *Discovery* returned to the city that made her and, on 3 April 1986, she docked in Dundee to a very warm welcome. Since then she has become the focus of a superb museum at Discovery Point.

226

FLESHER • TAILOR • CORDINER • WEAVER • DYER • HAMMERMAN • BONNET MAKER • BAKER • GLOVER •

DUNDEE SHIPBUILDING COMPANY

LAUNCHED
21ST MARCH 1901

THE DISCOVERY SAILS FROM DUNDEE

PANEL 114 Dundee, Jute, Jam and Journalism

Panel stitched by:

3J

Eleanor Arthur
Margaret Purvis
Marilyn Rattray
Alister Rutherford
Jessie Sword

Stitched in:
Broughty Ferry, Dundee

Dundee is very old and its name probably derives from *Dun-Deagh*, 'Fire Hill'. This may have been a reference to the early habit of fires being lit on hills on the old Celtic quarter days. It is also appropriate since it was the fire of the industrial revolution that made Dundee grow into the fourth largest city in Scotland. Jute and whales were the stimulus. A vegetable fibre imported from India, jute was tough but hard to spin. Whale oil, a by-product of the city's other industry, was found to lubricate this process very well and the manufacture of many jute-based products such as canvas, sacking and twine began. In 1797, Janet Keiller invented marmalade. Without doubt. Other unlikely sources of early recipes for this excellent product have been put forward but none convince. But marmalade and jam, made from the fruits of the nearby berry fields, made Dundee famous – as did Oor Wullie and Desperate Dan. Generations were raised on the characters of *The Beano*, *The Dandy* and *The Sunday Post*. All were owned by DC Thomson, an enormously prolific and influential publishing company based in the city. One of the best but least remembered creations of the artists and writers at DC Thomson was Black Bob. This strip about a Border collie sheepdog and shepherd Andrew Glen, his alleged owner, ran in *The Weekly News* until 1967. Both are still missed.

PANEL 115 Shetland, the Isbister Sisters

Panel stitched by:

Pentland Stitches

Ali Cameron
Sara-Jayne Donaldson
Angela E. Lewis
Meg Macleod
Ann Mair
Carmel Ross

Stitched in:
Thurso, Dunnet, Caithness

In rural communities all over Scotland women worked hard, doing menial, muscular tasks that would perhaps surprise modern sensibilities. On farms men did everything associated with horses – ploughing, carting, harvesting – while women did the back-breaking work of weeding, shawing, milking and bringing fuel for the fire. This everyday portrait of two sisters shows them with peat creels on their backs, chatting as they walk, knitting without a glance at what their practised fingers are doing. The exodus from the land of the last century has rendered much of what used to be thought of women's work redundant as well as changing its traditional meaning. Washing the dishes does not compare to weeding a field of turnips in the rain.

PANEL 116 Charles Rennie Mackintosh

Panel stitched by:

The Dotty Stitchers

Irene Mitchell
Lindsay Morrison
Marion Nimmo
Christine Rettig
Kate Ross
Dorothy Stalker
Sue Whitaker
Susan Wylie

Stitched in:
Erskine, Glasgow, Clydebank,
Renfrewshire

Built between 1897 and 1908, the Glasgow School of Art made the international reputation of Charles Rennie Mackintosh, Scotland's greatest artist. Trained as an architect, he, nevertheless, designed virtually every element of the houses and institutions he had built, from the cutlery to the door furniture and the fabrics used for curtains. Later in life, he also revealed himself as a superb watercolourist of landscapes and flowers. Mackintosh worked closely with his wife, Margaret Macdonald, and she occasionally created gesso panels for his domestic commissions. The Glasgow School of Art is his greatest achievement. Built on an awkward sloping site and difficult to see from any distance, it is a triumph of invention and appropriateness. With the support of the school's headmaster, Francis Henry 'Fra' Newbery, Mackintosh was given great freedom and he expressed himself with brilliance. The library is a masterpiece. But, aside from two major domestic commissions, a school and a church, Mackintosh's prodigious talents were not used to the full partly because the First World War halted most building projects and partly for personal reasons. He left Glasgow to live first in London (and occasionally in Suffolk) and then in south-west France. Recalling his remarkable talent, the daughter of Fra Newbery, Mary Newbery Sturrock said, in the 1980s, that she wept at the waste of such an artist. 'I'd like to have seen his fiftieth house – it wouldn't have been a bit like the first.'

CHARLES RENNIE MACKINTOSH
DESIGNS GLASGOW SCHOOL OF ART

The Munros

Panel stitched by:

Joan Kerr

Stitched in:
Fort William

Non-Gaelic speakers may have difficulty in pronouncing the names of Scotland's mountains, but thanks to Sir Hugh Munro, we know how many of them rise to over 3,000 feet – 282. But there is also a classification known as a Munro Top, a summit that is not seen as a separate mountain, perhaps part of a ridge. There are 227 of them. Munro bagging has become a popular pastime. More than 4,000 have climbed them all but the number who have scaled more than a few must be much higher. Ben Nevis is probably the most famous Munro, being the highest mountain in Britain, but, with the constant traffic up and down, is it being worn down?

PANEL 118 The 1914–1918 War

Panel stitched by:

EH6 Group

Sorrell Bentinck
Alison Black
Andrea Bloomfield
Lucinda Byatt
Cherry Campbell
Fiona Campbell Byatt
Sarah Conlon
Karen Howlett
Naomi Jennings
Yoshiko Nakano
Alison Roarty

Stitched in:
Edinburgh

The slaughter of the First World War is commemorated on memorials all over Scotland. Impossibly long lists of the names of young men who died between 1914 and 1918 remember an unparalleled death toll. Few understood why Britain was at war with Germany, Austria and Turkey but any dissent was buried by patriotic zeal. Young men not in uniform, for whatever reason, risked having a white feather pinned to them by women who called them cowards. Men who had been wounded were given special badges to avoid such humiliation. As the war stagnated in the mud of Flanders and the death toll spiralled, Scotland suffered disproportionately with perhaps as many as a quarter of all Scots who fought being killed. The commander of the British Expeditionary Force from 1915 to 1918 was Field Marshal Douglas Haig, the 1st Earl Haig of Bemersyde. Born in Edinburgh in 1861, he became a regular soldier who rose through the ranks to great eminence. But, since the 1960s, his reputation has been attacked, with some historians recalling the label 'Butcher Haig' and criticising him for the needless slaughter of soldiers. Others have defended Haig, arguing that his strategy was ultimately successful. Certainly the experience of the trenches changed politicians' view of what a conscript army would and would not do, especially in the Second World War. There would be no repeat of the casualty lists of 1914–1918 where a staggering 4 per cent of British men were killed.

1914 - 1918 WAR

PANEL 119
The Building of HMS *Hood*, the Battle of Ypres 1917

Panel stitched by:

The Appin Stitchers

Joy Blakeney
Jean Breckenridge
Helen Currie
Doreen Evans
Janet Fairbairn
Midge Gourlay
Fiona Hunter
Margaret Rayworth
Morag White
Anne White
Pat Wyeth Webb

Stitched in:
Appin, Port Appin,
Benderloch, Barcaldine

Passchendaele has become a byword for the miseries of fighting in the trenches of Flanders. Also known as the Third Battle of Ypres, it was an offensive launched by the Allies to gain control of the ridges to the south and east of the Belgian city of Ypres. Lloyd George, the prime minister, was against the operation as was General Foch, the French commander. They wanted to wait for American reinforcement. But Field Marshal Haig persisted with the strategy of attacking in the west and approval was granted in July 1917. The human cost was vast and the gains negligible. Wet weather bogged down the advance, the German Fourth Army fought back strongly and ultimately British and French troops had to be deployed to Italy to shore up that front after an Austrian victory at Caporetto. If the land war was a stalemate, Britain hoped to win the war at sea and, on 1 September 1916, the keel of HMS *Hood* was laid down on Clydeside. Designated as a battlecruiser, *Hood* was huge and very heavily armed, outgunning the *Mackensen*-class German equivalents. She carried eight 42-calibre guns that could launch a 1,920-pound shell over a range of 17 miles at maximum elevation. Known as the *Mighty Hood*, she was not commissioned until 1920. More than 20 years later, this huge battlecruiser fought in one of the most famous naval engagements of the Second World War, the Battle of the Denmark Strait. The *Hood* was sunk by the *Prinz Eugen* and the *Bismarck* with an explosion in her magazines causing enormous loss of life. Out of a crew of 1,148, only three survived.

PACK UP YOUR TROUBLES IN YOUR OLD KIT BAG AND SMILE, SMILE, SMILE

THE BUILDING OF HMS HOOD, BATTLE OF YPRES 1917

Appin Stitchers

PANEL 120 Elsie Inglis

Panel stitched by:

Fiona Kirton
Jo Macrae
Deborah Ramage

Stitched in:
Edinburgh

One of the first female doctors to qualify, Elsie Inglis set up in medical practice in 1894 and opened a maternity hospital in Edinburgh. She was very unhappy with the standard of medical care for women and that propelled her into the women's suffrage movement. Elsie Inglis did pioneering work during the First World War but died in 1917 on her return to Britain. The Elsie Inglis Memorial Maternity Hospital was founded in Edinburgh and it continued to innovate in midwifery. It seemed that the consideration, warmth and humanity of its inspiration lasted for generations. The closure of the Elsie Inglis in 1988 may have made sense to some but its passing was much mourned by many.

The Sinking of HMY *Iolaire* off Stornoway, 1919

Panel stitched by:

Sea-Mistresses

Tracey MacLeod
Moira MacPherson
Gillian Scott-Forest

Stitched in:
Harris, South Uist

On the evening of 31 December 1918, the Admiralty yacht, HMY *Iolaire* (the name means 'Eagle' in Gaelic) sailed out of Kyle of Lochalsh bound for Stornoway on the Isle of Lewis. On board were 280 sailors returning home, having survived the horrors of the First World War. Within sight of the twinkling lights of the harbour, the yacht struck the infamous Beasts of Holm, a reef only twenty yards from the shore. In heaving seas, the yacht began to break up and 205 men were drowned, 181 of them Lewismen. In a small island community, the impact of this tragedy was huge. Only 75 survived and many of them because of the bravery and strength of John F. MacLeod of Ness. He swam ashore with a line, wrapped it around himself and about 40 men pulled themselves to safety along it. No satisfactory explanation for the disaster was ever produced and the legacy of the *Iolaire* is still felt. In 1958, a memorial was erected at Holm and a stone pillar built on the Beasts.

THE SINKING OF HMY IOLAIRE OFF STORNOWAY 1919

PANEL 122 Eric Liddell

Panel stitched by:

The Liberton Connection

Rosemary Leask
Sheila MacIsaac

Stitched in:
Edinburgh

The romantic days of amateur sport have no better exemplar than Eric Liddell. The Flying Scotsman won a gold medal for the 400 metres at the Paris Olympic Games of 1924, having refused, on religious grounds, to run on a Sunday in the heats for the 100 metres, his better event. His idiosyncratic running style, with his head flung back, his mouth wide open and his arms flailing, was remembered by all who saw him but it was his blistering speed that dazzled. His rival, Harold Abrahams, defended Liddell, saying, 'People may shout their heads off about his appalling style. Well, let them. He gets there.' The year before the Olympic Games, he had played rugby for Scotland. And, at the age of 23, he retired from sport so that he could become a missionary in China. Interned by the Japanese, Liddell died in 1945, probably of a brain tumour and malnourishment. But his achievements were never forgotten and they were immortalised in the Oscar-winning film, *Chariots of Fire*. When the great Scottish sprinter, Allan Wells, won Olympic gold in Moscow in 1980, he dedicated his race to the memory of Eric Liddell.

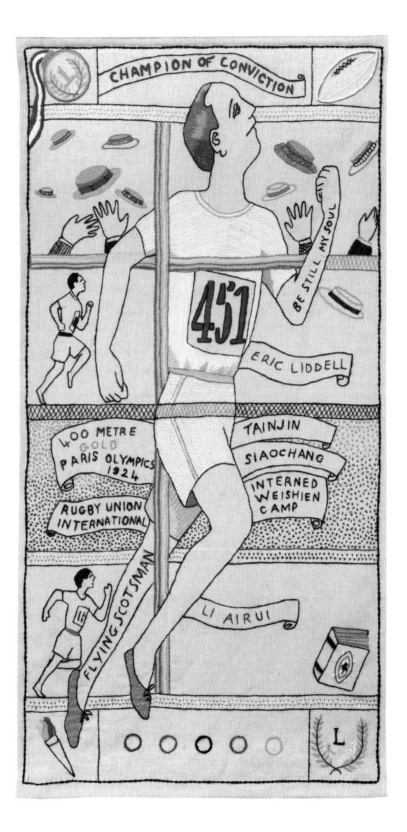

PANEL 123   # Women Get the Vote

Panel stitched by:

*Soroptimist International
of Edinburgh*

Edith Elliot
Jane Green
Clephane Hume
Winifred Keeves
Isabel Smith

Stitched in:
Dalkeith, Edinburgh

Elsie Inglis became a founder member of the Scottish Women's Suffragette Federation in 1906 and worked hard to see the franchise extended. Others were even more militant and Flora Drummond, a postmistress, went to prison nine times as a leader of the Women's Social and Political Union. Some poured acid into pillar boxes, slashed portraits of the king and set fire to buildings such as Ayr Racecourse, Leuchars Railway Station and the Whitekirk in East Lothian. In prison, many went on hunger strikes. The First World War supplied unexpected support as suffragettes suspended campaigning. While men fought and died on the Western Front in their millions, many women worked in the munitions industries, joined the Women's Land Army or drove buses and ambulances. All were seen in a different light as a result. New legislation was enacted in 1918 to give all women over the age of 30 the right to vote in general elections and to stand as MPs. But pressure for equality did not abate and, in 1928, women 21 and over were allowed to vote.

PERTH PRISON | JESSIE STEPHEN | McPHUN SISTERS | BALMORAL GOLF COURSE | ST. MARYS, WHITEKIRK

FOR VALOUR

HUNGER STRIKE

FLORA DRUMMOND ETHEL MOORHEAD

ELSIE INGLIS

GRACE CADELL

DEEDS NOT WORDS

A GUDE CAUSE MAKS A STRONG ARM

WOMEN GET THE VOTE

S.I. EDINBURGH

PANEL 124 Whaling

Panel stitched by:

Rebecca Fish
Alasdair Fish
Rosalind Neville-Smith
Joyce Peace
Hazel Shearer
Molly Shearer
Leah Shearer

Stitched in:
Orkney

Demand for whale oil for use in lighting drove a major expansion in whaling. Out of ports such as Dundee and Peterhead, whaling ships sailed the Arctic but overfishing seriously depleted stocks. In the early 20th century, Christian Salvesen established a whaling station in Shetland as well as one in the Antarctic on the island of South Georgia. Salvesen became the largest whaling company in the world in part because of their pioneering use of the entire carcass of the whale. By the end of the 20th century, stocks had dwindled so alarmingly that a complete moratorium had to be imposed to allow species to recover.

PANEL 125 The General Strike, 1926

Panel stitched by:

Big County Gals

June McEwan
Karen Phillpot
Gill Tulloch

Stitched in:
Pitlochry

Lasting only nine days, the strike was called by the Trades Union Congress in an attempt to force the government to halt a downward spiral of wages and conditions for 800,000 miners. More than 1.7 million workers downed tools. In the face of well-laid preparations and the support of the middle classes, students and others in maintaining services, the General Strike failed. Instead of building a land fit for heroes after the First World War, there was unemployment and deprivation, a broken promise to those who survived the trenches or lost relatives. In Glasgow, huge crowds gathered and soldiers were mobilised. The Riot Act was read from Glasgow City Chambers and the police charged demonstrators. But the left-wing MPs, Mannie Shinwell and Willie Gallacher, had no coherent political plan apart from protest and nothing of any real consequence was achieved. The strike was called off without any guarantees, terms or even a written statement. Such abject surrender was greeted with a mixture of fury and disgust in Glasgow.

GENERAL STRIKE 1926

PANEL 126 Fair Isle

Panel stitched by:

Marietta di Ciacca
Edna Elliott-McColl
Susan Finlayson

Stitched in:
Port Seton

Midway between Shetland and Orkney, Fair Isle is small, sparsely populated and famous. In 1900, the population was 400 but now it numbers only 70 and most live in the crofts on the southern part of the island. It is famous in the shipping forecast and for a traditional style of knitting. The latter became popular when the Prince of Wales, later to reign briefly as Edward VIII, took to wearing Fair Isle knitted sleeveless jumpers to play golf in the early 1920s. Very colourful and with finely worked horizontal geometric patterns, these designs consequently became the acme of fashion. And they are still are.

FAIR
ISLE
KNITTING

PANEL 127 Hugh MacDiarmid

Panel stitched by:

The Albyn Stitchers

Barbara Gregor
Linda Herd
Diana Herriot
Samantha Townsend

Stitched in:
Livingston

Hugh MacDiarmid's masterpiece, *A Drunk Man Looks at the Thistle* incorporates a passage on the General Strike – a pessimistic response to its failure. The great lyric is a montage of invective and humour and a collection of themes dealt with in what seem like distinct poems. But it has an authentic voice in Scots – something MacDiarmid imbibed in his youth in the Borders town of Langholm. It begins:

> I amna fou sae muckle as tired – deid dune.
> It's gey and hard wark coupin' gless for gless
> Wi' Cruivie and Gilsanquhar and the like,
> And I'm no' juist as bauld as aince I wes.

Christened Christopher Murray Grieve, MacDiarmid was born in Langholm in 1892 and he led a deeply individual life. During the 1930s, he was expelled from the Communist Party for being a Scottish Nationalist and then expelled from the Scottish National Party for being a communist. And, in 1956, when Soviet tanks invaded Hungary, he rejoined the Communist Party. Living in abject poverty, scraping a living with journalism, MacDiarmid worked tirelessly as a poet and writer and happily admitted that his work was of variable quality. But he was undoubtedly a Scottish literary genius, enormously influential, thrawn and indefatigable. When MacDiarmid died in 1978, his fellow poet, Norman MacCaig, suggested that each year the great man's passing be celebrated by two minutes' pandemonium.

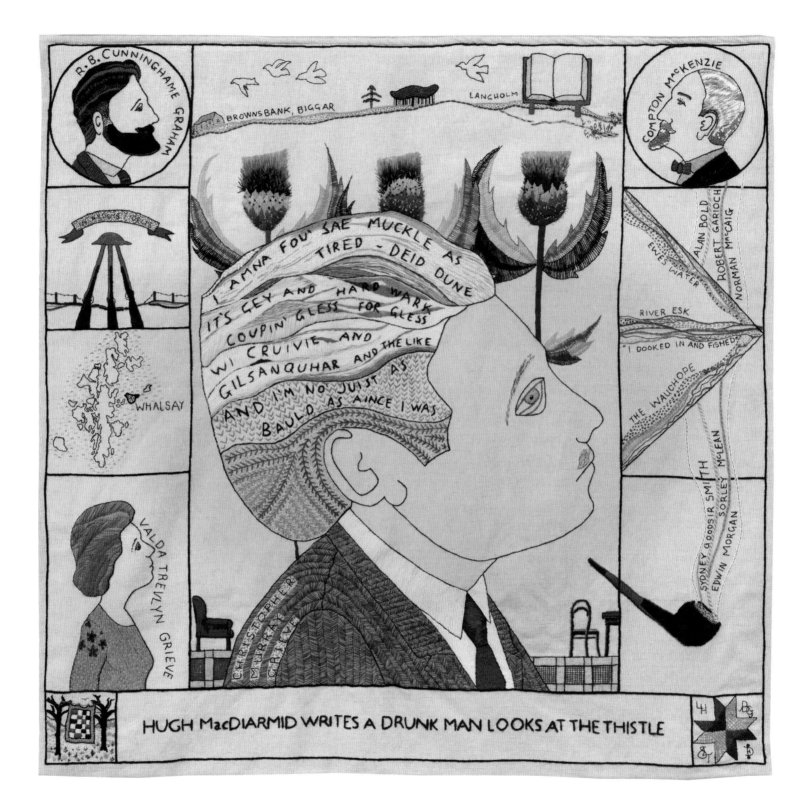

R.B. CUNNINGHAME GRAHAM

COMPTON MACKENZIE

BROWNSBANK, BIGGAR

LANGHOLM

WHALSAY

VALDA TREVLYN GRIEVE

I AMNA FOU' SAE MUCKLE AS
TIRED - DEID DUNE
IT'S GEY AND HARD WARK
COUPIN' GLESS FOR GLESS
WI' CRUIVIE AND
GILSANQUHAR AND THE LIKE
AND I'M NO JUIST AS
BAULD AS AINCE I WAS

CHRISTOPHER MURRAY GRIEVE

ALAN BOLD
ROBERT GARIOCH
NORMAN MacCAIG
EWES WATER
RIVER ESK
"I DOOKED IN AND FISHED"
THE WAUCHOPE
SYDNEY GOODSIR SMITH
SORLEY McLEAN
EDWIN MORGAN

HUGH MacDIARMID WRITES A DRUNK MAN LOOKS AT THE THISTLE

Ramsay MacDonald and the Rise of the Labour Party

Panel stitched by:

Jenny Allan
Polly Atkinson
Joan Bell
Ariane Burgess
Amanda Cooper
Corinne Davies
Rian Davies
Isabel di Sotto
Jenny Doig
Daphne Francis
Anne Gavin
Mary Haslam
Jacqui Hassan
Katyi Hassan
Linda Jones
Wilma MacBain
Fiona MacDonald
Marjorie Macleod
Joyce MacNaught
Shiela McCourt
Diane McGregor
Anne Milligan
Katherine Murray
Judi O'May
Frances Powell
Kathleen Purmal
Linda Robertson
Kathleen Ross
Anne Skene
Wendy Springett
Yvonne Stuart
Davina Thomas
June Watson
James Watson

Stitched in:
Burghead, Forres, Findhorn

The first Labour Prime Minister was a Scot, Ramsay MacDonald. The illegitimate son of a farm labourer, John MacDonald and a housemaid, Anne Ramsay, he was raised and educated in Lossiemouth. In 1906, he was elected to the House of Commons as a Labour MP for Leicester and, in 1911, he became party leader. Implacably opposed to the First World War, he lost his seat in 1918 but returned to parliament in 1922 in the general election that saw Labour replace the Liberals as the second largest party. And, into the 1920s, MacDonald's pacifism and his oratorical skills earned him the respect of the electorate. By the early 1920s, Labour had become the main opposition party to the Conservatives and, in 1924, King George V called on him to form a minority government with the support of the Liberal Party. It only lasted nine months but showed that Labour had the ability to govern credibly. In 1929, MacDonald and Labour returned to government as the largest party but were overwhelmed by the onset of the Great Depression. When he formed a National Government, MacDonald was expelled from the Labour Party but carried on as prime minister. In 1931, he won a huge majority and Labour's Westminster representation was reduced to a rump of only 50 seats. Prime minister on three separate occasions, he stood down in 1935, losing his seat in the election (but becoming MP for the Combined Scottish Universities in a by-election a year later) and two years later MacDonald resigned as his physical and mental health collapsed. From a single-parent family living in a cottage in Lossiemouth to 10 Downing Street – it was an astonishingly meteoric life course for the time.

FIRST LABOUR PRIME MINISTER

1 GREGORY PLACE
LOSSIEMOUTH

IS THERE FOR HONEST POVERTY

A MAN'S A MAN FOR A' THAT

RAMSAY MACDONALD PRIME MINISTER RISE OF THE LABOUR PARTY

FINDHORN / FORRES

BURGHEAD CRAFT GROUP

PANEL 129 The Great Depression

Panel stitched by:

Kelly's Cats

Audrey Anderson
Pat Balfour
Mary Bibby
Alison Black
Heather Bramwell
Nan Chalmers
Heather King
Margaret Moir
Gail Neiman
Kay Paul
Olive Pauline
Alison Purvis
Margaret Ruddiman
Maureen Stuchbury
June Willox
Verna Wilson

Stitched in:
Aberdeen

When Wall Street crashed and confidence evaporated in the American economy in late 1929, the effects ricocheted around the world. And, unlike in 2008, there was no international consensus on how to effect recovery. Britain's world trade fell by half, unemployment soared to 3.5 million and the output of heavy industry plunged by a third. Scotland was particularly affected by the latter. But, because there had been no post-war boom to speak of in the 1920s, the slump was less extreme than it was in North America. However, the Scottish coalfields saw many men laid off as demand dried up and shipbuilding was badly hit on the Clyde. In 1931, unemployment benefit was paid according to need rather than contributions made but it was contingent on a means test and this was the cause of bitter resentment. A deep north–south split became apparent in Britain. A recovery began slowly in the south where house-building offered employment but the heavy industries and mining in Scotland, on Tyneside and in Yorkshire and Lancashire and Wales remained depressed. And the widespread resentment at Conservative economic policies began to store up a wish for change that erupted in the surprising general election result of 1945. But what began to send men and women back to work in the heavy industries of the north was the government decision to rearm in the face of Nazi aggression.

A SCOTS QUAIR

SUNSET SONG

CLOUD HOWE

GREY GRANITE

IT'S A SAIR FECHT

FOR A HALF-LOAF

GREAT DEPRESSION IN 1930s

PANEL 130 Tenement Life

Panel stitched by:

Paisley Patter

Marie Connelly
Gladys Connolly
Carla Corneli
Natalie Elliott
Liz Gardiner
Christine Gilmour
Irene Harvey
Lesley King
Aga Kulet
Catherine Lappin
Morven McAlister
Margaret McBride
Paula McKeown
Margaret Muir
Anne Ross
Grant Scott
Jan Walker
Rita Winters
Michaela Wright

Stitched in:
Paisley, Elderslie, Greenock,
Glasgow

As a solution to the density of urban living, tenements are ancient. In Rome and the great cities of the ancient world, multi-occupancy in buildings of several storeys was common. In industrialising England, the term soon acquired a pejorative gloss since it meant overcrowding and slum conditions, but in Scotland tenement life could be very attractive to working people. Even though shared toilets on the stair-heid were the norm, and the drying green and entrance were communal, the neighbourliness and mutual support, especially in hard times, usually more than compensated. Densely packed communities produced their own entertainment and social and sporting clubs thrived. As did political discourse. One of the greatest products of the Paisley tenements was Willie Gallacher, a founder of the Communist Party of Great Britain who was MP for West Fife between 1935 and 1950. In the slum clearances of the 1960s and 70s tenements were demolished and replaced with tower blocks. Which in turn were demolished and replaced with – tenements. This time with their own toilets.

IN 1930 I WAS A DREAMER

I WORKED SO HARD ALL OF THE TIME

BUT I WAS ALWAYS HAPPY

PAISLEY

RUSSELL INSTITUTE

KELBURNE

J&P COATS
ONE MILE 40 ONE MILE

WILLIE GALLACHER

Anchor

The Second World War

Panel stitched by:

JHEMMS

Marion Harkins
Joan Marsh
Susan Matthew
Heather Neal
Eileen Rennie
Mary Woodward

Stitched in:
Edinburgh, Musselburgh

The first action of the Second World War was fought in the skies above the Firth of Forth as German aircraft attacked the naval base at Rosyth. Several were shot down. Scapa Flow in Orkney was also strategically vital for the North Atlantic and Shetland's proximity to Norway gave rise to the Shetland bus, a series of voyages by fishing boats to help Norwegians flee the Nazi invasion and aid their resistance efforts. Scots were notable in operations with Air Chief Marshal Hugh Dowding from Moffat leading Fighter Command and Robert Watson Watt's invention of radar giving defenders the edge in the Battle of Britain in 1940. Col. David Stirling founded the SAS, the Special Air Service. He was eventually captured and sent to Colditz Castle. But perhaps the most significant incarceration was the surrender and capture of the 51st Highland Division at St Valery. After the defeat of the British Expeditionary Force and the evacuation from Dunkirk, bad weather forced General Fortune to capitulate. For most of the duration of the war, they were held at Stalag XX-A in Poland and, in 1945, forced to march 450 miles west to Luneberg Heath, north of Hanover. On the home front, Prof. John Raeburn from Aberdeen was an agricultural economist who organised the 'Dig For Victory' campaign that fed Britain between 1939 and 1945. He encouraged people to convert lawns and flowerbeds into allotments and to keep chickens and pigs in back gardens. More than 900 'pig clubs' sprang up and, with rationing, it is said that Britain has never had as healthy a diet as it did during the Second World War.

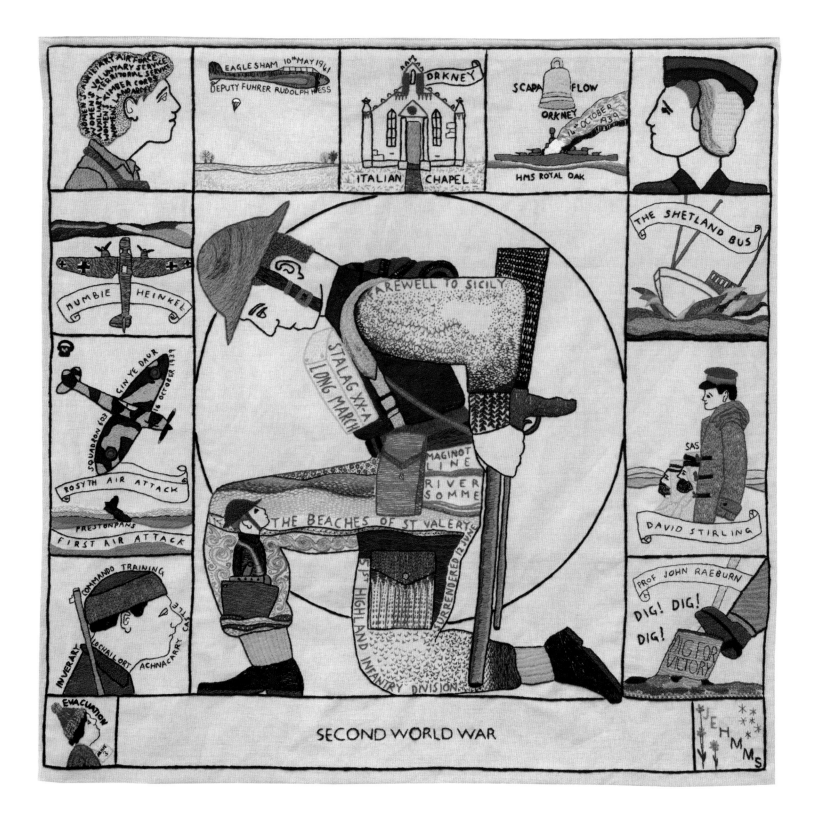

SECOND WORLD WAR

PANEL 132   The Clydebank Blitz

Panel stitched by:

Nervous Needles

Shona Glenn
Claire McDonald
Carole Ross
Marjorie Sinclair

Stitched in:
Edinburgh

In March 1941, the Luftwaffe mounted two devastating raids on Clydebank and its shipbuilding yards. The town was destroyed and 528 people lost their lives, a further 617 were seriously injured and many were hurt by blast debris. Out of approximately 12,000 houses, 4,000 were completely destroyed and 4,500 severely damaged, making 35,000 people homeless. But the major targets of the John Brown shipyard and Beardmore's Diesel Works were not badly hit and were able to continue to function. The German raid was vast, with 439 bombers dropping more than 1,000 bombs. Only two were shot down by the RAF but the guns of the Polish destroyer, *Piorun*, helped defend the town from the docks as it fired at the aircraft. There is a war memorial in Clydebank dedicated to the bravery of the Polish sailors. The attack took place over two nights and the damage to housing in the first raid was collateral since most of the workers lived close to the yards and the plants. But the following night seems to have been a terror raid aimed at civilians in an effort to damage not only their houses but also their morale. It failed.

THE CLYDEBANK BLITZ 1941

PANEL 133   War Defences

Panel stitched by:

May Bowie
Patsy Brown
Frances Fettes

Stitched in:
North Berwick, Eskbank

Several generations after the German surrender, the marks of war can still be found in Scotland. When an invasion fleet sailed up the Oslo Fjord in 1940, one of its strategic aims was to open up a thousand-mile-long start line for an invasion of Britain. That, in turn, exposed the east coast of Scotland to a direct threat of invasion. Concrete obstacles to inhibit tank movement were hurriedly built on beaches and pillboxes set up at strategic vantage points. But, while the nearest and clearest threat was to the south-east of England, Scotland had few soldiers to defend its shores. In many places, a German invasion force could have landed unchallenged. The Moray Firth coastlands were thought to be particularly vulnerable and so the Cowie Stop Line was constructed. Near Stonehaven and following the line of the Cowie Water, a series of earthworks and concrete obstacles was built between the North Sea coastline and the foothills of the Grampians. This narrow neck of land was the gateway to southern Scotland and, while invaders might have been able to land in Moray or Banff, they would have had to round that corner of Scotland's geography. In truth, the Cowie Stop Line would have slowed down an advance rather than halt it. In the 1950s and 1960s, Scotland's concrete defences against the Nazis supplied schoolchildren with a setting for war games with toy guns that had more than a shiver of authenticity. They were built for a real war and might really have been attacked.

CRAMOND

PORTKNOCKIE

CRUDEN BAY

LUNAN BAY

TENTS MUIR

BURNTISLAND

PORT SETON

DREM

1ST POLISH ARMY CORP

POLISH-SCOTTISH ASSOCIATION 1940-42

PANEL 134 D-Day, 1944

Panel stitched by:

Margaret Burgess
Olive McCrone
Anne Ratigan
Caroline Scott
Nicki Slater
Alison Wood

Stitched in:
Edinburgh, Winchburgh

On 6 June 1944, the largest amphibious invasion ever mounted landed on the beaches of Normandy to begin the reconquest of Nazi Europe. More than 73,000 American soldiers, 61,715 British and 21,400 Canadians either splashed ashore under heavy fire or were parachuted in the night before. Known as Operation Overlord, the landings saw some of the fiercest fighting of the Second World War. Scotland had not only been involved in the preparations and training for the landings, many Scottish soldiers attempted to fight their way up the beaches. Simon Fraser, Lord Lovat, commanded 1 Special Service Brigade and he instructed his personal piper, Bill Millin, to play as the troops landed. Under heavy German fire, he played 'The Road to the Isles' and 'Hielan' Laddie'. The piper was the only soldier in the Normandy Landings to wear a kilt – a Cameron tartan worn by his father in the trenches in the First World War. Apart from his sgian-dubh sheathed in his socks, Millan carried no weapons. Later, he talked to captured German snipers who said that they did not shoot at him because they thought he was crazy. Lovat's brigade advanced to Pegasus Bridge, bravely defended by the Ox and Bucks Light Infantry, with Millin leading and playing the pipes. Twelve men wearing berets were shot through the head and commandos then raced across the bridge with helmets on. In 2009, Piper Millin was decorated by the French government, receiving the Croix d'Honneur for gallantry.

HIGHLAND LIGHT INFANTRY

ARGYLL AND SUTHERLAND HIGHLANDERS

BLACK WATCH

QUEEN'S OWN CAMERON HIGHLANDERS

KING'S OWN SCOTTISH BORDERERS

FIFE AND FORFAR YEOMANRY

GORDON HIGHLANDERS

SEAFORTH HIGHLANDERS

ROYAL SCOTS FUSILIERS

CAMERONIANS

FORTITUDE NORTH

518 SQUADRON TIREE

ATLANTIC BRIDGE

CAIRNRYAN & FASLANE CLYDE

No.1 COMBINED TRAINING CENTRE INVERARAY

ROYAL SCOTS GREYS

OPERATION

OVERLORD

TALISMAN

FLOATING MULBERRY HARBOUR

X CRAFT

D-DAY 1944

Anne Ratigan
Alison Wood
Nicki Slater

Caroline Scott
Olive McCrone
Margaret Burgess

PANEL 135 The First Edinburgh Festival

Panel stitched by:

Festival Group

Jo Allen
Ann Campbell
Mairi Campbell
Heather Davidson
Alice Henderson
Eleanor Horton
Jackie Kemp
Jan Kerr
Le-Anne Koh
Sue Lougheed
Delia Marriott
Janis McGravie
Moira Nelson
Kirstin Norrie
Sigridur Oladottir
Ffion Reville
Fiona Roche
Patsy Seddon
Heather Swinson
Linda Swinson
Margareta Thomson
Catriona White
Lois Yelland

Stitched in:
Dalkeith, Port Seton,
Edinburgh, Gorebridge,
Eddleston

Grim austerity followed the end of the Second World War but one sparkling innovation lit the gloom. In 1947, the first Edinburgh Festival took place. The brainchild of Rudolf Bing, the director of Glyndebourne Opera and Lord Provost Sir John Falconer, it brought orchestras, ballet, theatre and exhibitions to the city each August. The official festival programme was immediately joined by the Festival Fringe – eight groups who wanted to add their largely amateur performances. Apparently, 1947 saw a warm and sunny summer, something which added greatly to the atmosphere of optimism. The Fringe has come to dominate the Edinburgh Festival and it is now the largest and best arts festival in the world. It operates like no other. Performers may join the Festival Fringe Society, hire a venue and put on a show. There is no central artistic control and this openness has been the stimulus for the successful beginning of many brilliant careers, from the playwright Tom Stoppard, through the Cambridge Footlights of 1981, with Stephen Fry, Hugh Laurie, Emma Thompson and Tony Slattery, to the brilliant impressionist Rory Bremner. Cultural entrepreneurs have begun to exercise a degree of selection and few have had the impact of Bill Burdett-Coutts over the last 30 years with Assembly Productions. Collectively, as Beethoven is played alongside stand-up comedy and the Scotsman Fringe First Awards for new drama are up for grabs, Edinburgh is simply the best place to be in August – in the world. No question.

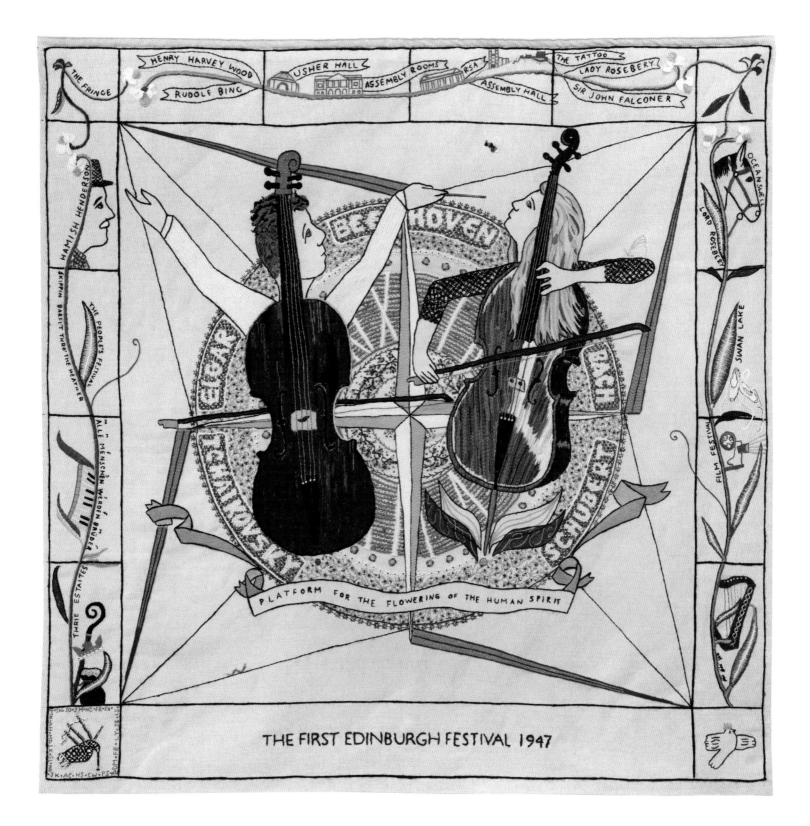

THE FIRST EDINBURGH FESTIVAL 1947

PANEL 136 East Kilbride and the New Towns

Panel stitched by:

Sandy Andrew
Ann Arnot
Sandra Douglas
Joanna Young

Stitched in:
Eskbank, Edinburgh,
West Linton

On 6 May 1947 East Kilbride was designated as Scotland's first new town. Overcrowded housing in Glasgow was a stimulus for the Clyde Valley Regional Plan and it envisaged satellite new towns and peripheral housing estates to relieve pressure. Planners created neighbourhoods in East Kilbride, each with local shops, services and primary schools, and in the centre was a series of linked malls. When the first residents came, it must have seemed like the New Jerusalem. The old, decrepit tenements of Glasgow, with shared toilets, vermin and a cheek-by-jowl existence were replaced with houses with proper bathrooms and heating. East Kilbride has grown to a population of almost 74,000. In 1948, Glenrothes was founded around a mine that never fully functioned, but that source of employment was replaced by the introduction of major electronics companies. To the east of Glasgow, Cumbernauld was founded in 1956 and, near Edinburgh, Livingston in 1962. Irvine completed Scotland's five new towns in 1964.

EAST KILBRIDE 1947

A TOWN FOR TOMORROW

CLYDE VALLEY REGIONAL PLAN 1943

Scotland's New Towns
1. East Kilbride   1947
2. Glenrothes   1948
3. Cumbernauld   1956
4. Livingston   1962
5. Irvine   1966

PANEL 137 The National Health Service

Panel stitched by:

Friends in Fine Embroidery

Lydia Lawson
June McAleece
Irene Wood

Stitched in:
Dunfermline, Dalgety Bay,
Kirkcaldy

Britain's greatest post-war achievement was the foundation of the National Health Service. This key element of the incoming Labour government's manifesto was difficult to deliver. Many doctors had been used to charging for their services and were unwilling to cooperate but Aneurin Bevan, the Minister of Health, later said he had 'stuffed their mouths with gold'. In his book, *In Place of Fear*, Bevan wrote that 'no society can legitimately call itself civilised if a sick person is denied medical aid because of a lack of means'. That remains the guiding principle of the NHS. The National Health Service (Scotland) Act brought the new service into being with the intention of care being free at the point of need. Some prescription charges were brought in and have continued in England but, in Scotland where healthcare is devolved, there are no such charges. With an ageing population living longer, the cost of the NHS in Scotland is rising and stood at £11.35 billion for 2010–2011. But the service is also Scotland's largest employer. In 2007, the Scottish government announced its opposition to partnerships between the NHS and the private sector and, a year later, it abolished the much-resented car parking charges at all hospitals except those funded by a private finance initiative scheme in Dundee, Edinburgh and Glasgow. The history of the NHS in Scotland is filled with remarkable statistics. In the year it was founded, around 500,000 Scots who needed them were prescribed spectacles and, partly due to consistent campaigning, the number of smokers in Scotland has declined from 80 per cent in 1954 to 23 per cent in 2011.

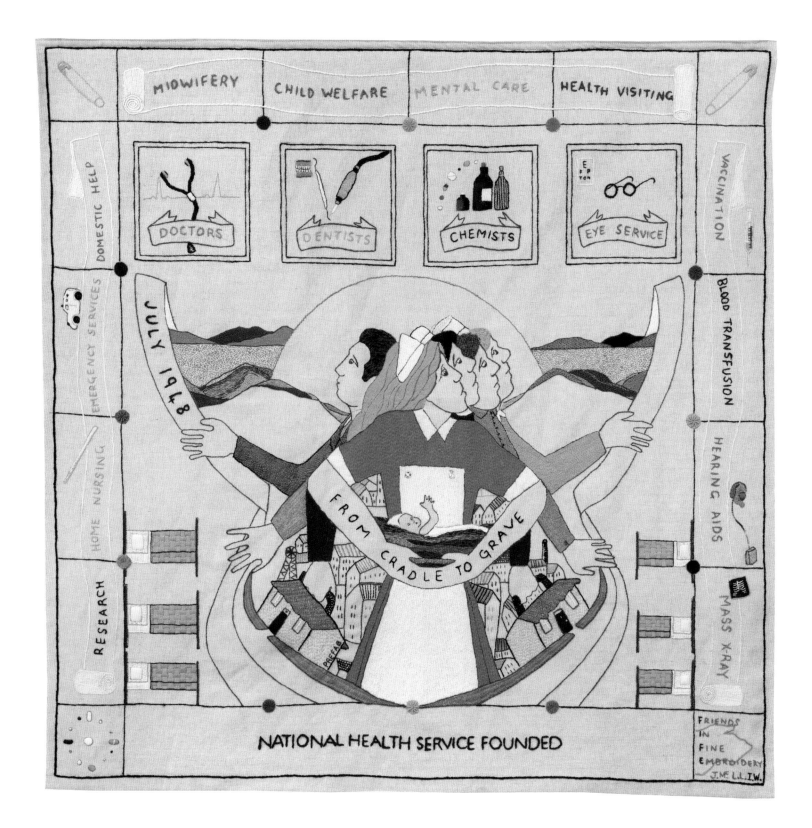

PANEL 138 Television Arrives

Panel stitched by:

Musselburgh Stitchers

Gaynor Allen
Susan Finlay
Sue Henderson
Rosemary Taylor

Stitched in:
Musselburgh

In the 1950s, the BBC's monopoly was broken with the introduction of ITV in Scotland. STV was first, launching in 1957, and its programmes were what one regulator called 'distressingly popular'. The *One O'Clock Gang* developed a devoted following and the programmes STV took from the other ITV companies soon out-rated the BBC's. Based in Glasgow, STV served the Central Belt and most of the population. Grampian Television set up in Aberdeen in 1961 and, to serve southern Scotland, Border Television began broadcasting from Carlisle in the same year. Diversity was the keynote as three separate daily news services were added to the BBC's national bulletins. And, as brands, STV, Grampian and Border were well recognised and well loved. They also supplied a local training ground for many behind and in front of the cameras. Many famous faces first appeared on *Scotland Today*, *North Tonight* or *Lookaround*. These three stations supplied a huge volume of local features, news and drama for about 40 years. But, when Prime Minister Margaret Thatcher decided that the ITV companies should make cash bids to renew their franchises and takeovers would be allowed, the old system began to disintegrate. Most of the invaluable regional coverage supplied by STV, Grampian and Border was swept away in a series of mergers and regulatory changes after 2008.

PANEL 139 The Washer Women

Panel stitched by:

Gail Hughes
Kate MacKenzie

Stitched in:
Montrose

As Scotland became more affluent and the cost of white goods in particular came within the reach of ordinary people, society shifted a little. Washing machines installed and operated at home effected one of the most striking changes. The 'steamies' or the communal washhouses began to close down. Before the coming of cheaper appliances, most women had taken their weekly wash to the steamie and these buildings, still recognisable in many towns and cities, were social hubs, part of the fabric of a neighbourhood. Also, professional washerwomen became redundant. And clothes probably became a little less well cleaned and pressed.

PANEL 140 Cumbernauld New Town

Panel stitched by:

Boulton + Conley

Elizabeth Boulton
Helen Conley

Stitched in:
Cumbernauld

The new town was originally designed without any pedestrian road crossings and was widely believed to be dominated by the needs of drivers rather then walkers. In 2002, Cumbernauld was voted the worst town in Scotland and, in 2005, its Town Centre won an unwanted public nomination for demolition in a Channel Four TV series. But action was taken. Parts of the Town Centre were indeed demolished and the housing stock's high quality was emphasised. And far from being a concrete jungle, Cumbernauld has space and greenery and the Campsie Fells can be seen from many places. In 2010, the new town was voted the most improved town in Scotland.

CUMBERNAULD NEW TOWN

PANEL 141 North Sea Oil

Panel stitched by:

Lundie

Catharina Dessain
Judy Drysdale
Katherine Ellvers
Susan Houstoun
Sylvia Learoyd
Susan Macgregor
Fiona Macphie
Georgie Middleton
Georgie Sampson
Caroline Southesk
Margaret Taylor
Griselda Thornton-Kemsley
Patsy Walker

Stitched in:
Forfar, Angus, Brechin,
Laurencekirk

In September 1965, a British Petroleum drilling rig found gas under the bed of the North Sea and, four years later, oil was also discovered. As the huge Brent and Forties fields came on stream, Britain began to enjoy an unlikely oil boom. Aberdeen became a city of business and high property prices while construction further north at Nigg Bay and terminals at Sullom Voe on Shetland have supplied employment. Linked by a 230km-long pipeline to the Piper and Occidental fields, Flotta on Orkney is also a major focus. Grangemouth is the centre of the petrochemical industry. Scotland became and remains the largest oil producer in the European Union and it is estimated that the industry employs more than 100,000, about 6 per cent of the total workforce. Production has begun to decline but vast reserves, perhaps 20 billion barrels, still remain under the chill waters of the North Sea. Most oil fields will remain in production until 2020 and, as oil prices rise, companies are very motivated to explore and exploit further. Teams have already been exploring more of the north-east Atlantic Basin around the Hebrides and to the west of Shetland – areas that were previously thought to be uneconomic.

SULLOM VOE

BON ACCORD

ST MACHAR'S

MONTROSE

BRENT

FORTIES

ARGYLL

NORTH SEA OIL LICENCES GRANTED 1965 ABERDEEN. NIGG BAY

PANEL 142 Aberdeen

Panel stitched by:

Inverdon Stitchers

Neil McMillan
Mary Middleton
Diane Stanley
Ursula Thompson

Stitched in:
Bridge of Don

For many centuries, Aberdeen has been a vibrant urban centre. Made a royal burgh by King David I between 1124 and 1153, it quickly became busy and, for the times, populous. Its situation at the mouth of the River Dee, with a harbour, good sea and land communications and facing a North Sea trading area all helped to make the city the third largest in Scotland by the 17th century. Uniquely, Aberdeen had two universities. King's College was founded in 1495 by Bishop William Elphinstone and, in 1593, Marischal College was endowed by George Keith, the Earl Marischal of Scotland. The two universities only united in 1860 and they are the fifth oldest in the English-speaking world. In the first half of the 19th century, Aberdeen redeveloped its harbour as the fishing and shipbuilding industries became busier. In the later 20th century, the oil industry once again filled the quaysides with ships that serviced the rigs and most oil companies run offices in the city. The impact on house prices has been marked. Perhaps one of the most glorious chapters in Aberdeen's history has been the phenomenal success of its football team under the management of Alex Ferguson. During Ferguson's reign, they won the Scottish League Premier Division three times, the Scottish Cup four times, The Scottish League Cup once and both the European Cup Winners' Cup and the European Super Cup in 1983.

PANEL 143 Linwood and the Hillman Imp

Panel stitched by:

Tillicoultry 'Needles & Gins'

Margaret Callander
Morag Clark
Shirley Galletly
Joan Gibson
Myra Legge
Gill Pritchard
Lesley Thornton

Stitched in:
Devonside, Alva, Tillicoultry,
Menstrie, Cambusbarron

Amongst the wreckage of Britain's once-vibrant car industry, the story of the Hillman Imp stands out. To compete with the Mini and find a niche as a second car for more affluent families, the Rootes Group took a huge gamble. Without much experience of building smaller cars, they built a huge new, computerised plant at Linwood, west of Glasgow, which opened on 2 May 1963. It lay close to a rail depot and its output could be transported quickly to showrooms all over Britain. But an early problem was that the railway was also needed to bring parts north from the Rootes plant at Ryton, near Coventry. Affordable, good-looking and innovative, the Imp initially sold well but it proved to be unreliable and sales dropped off. Half of the whole output of Imps were sold in the first three years of production. But it was seen as a Scottish car and continued to sell well north of the border. Rootes were bought by the American car maker, Chrysler, in 1967 but, despite price discounting, sales of the Imp declined. Production finally ceased in 1976 and, five years later, the Linwood plant closed. But Imps live on and models are lovingly cared for, many of them polished in Scottish garages.

RAVENSCRAIG

LINWOOD BEGINS PRODUCTION OF HILLMAN IMP

PANEL 144 Pop Music Booms

Panel stitched by:

Jacquie & The Juniors

Imogen Allen
Jacquie McNally
Charlie McNally

Stitched in:
Musselburgh

When the Beatles, the Rolling Stones and many other groups broke on to the popular music scene in the early 1960s, their success had at least two effects. First, it quickly became clear that young people were a separate market for much more than music. Fashion changed and very large numbers of teenagers and men and women in their twenties suddenly appeared to have spending power – enough money to create many new markets. The second effect was the worldwide success of British pop. It inspired a generation of Scottish musicians and singers. In contrast to the more traditional appeal of Kenneth McKellar and Moira Anderson, the likes of Donovan and Jack Bruce were genuine innovators. Born Donovan Leitch in Maryhill in Glasgow, his 'Catch the Wind' reached number 4 in the UK charts in 1965 and was followed by a string of hits on both sides of the Atlantic. Cream was the name of the band that included Jack Bruce, Eric Clapton and Ginger Baker. Their third album, *Wheels of Fire*, was the world's first platinum-selling double album. Others added to the variety of pop music coming out of Scotland, ranging from Lulu and the Bay City Rollers to the Incredible String Band.

POP MUSIC BOOMS

PANEL 145 Glenrothes

Panel stitched by:

The Coo's Tail

Ruby Henderson
Jan MacArthur
Patricia Macindoe
Mairi Stewart

Stitched in:
Old Kilpatrick,
Helensburgh, Glasgow

Having been established in central Fife to house miners who were to work at the new Rothes Colliery, this new town grew out of failure, prospered and became the administrative capital of the region. Opened by the Queen and designed as the first super-pit with state-of-the-art technology, the new colliery was supposed to produce 5,000 tons of coal a week but, beset by geological problems and flooding, it lasted only four years and closed in 1963. But Silicon Glen came to the rescue. A Scottish variant of Silicon Valley south of San Francisco, this was a collective name for the establishment of hi-tech industry in Scotland. In 1960, Hughes Aircraft opened its first factory outside of the USA to make semiconductors. It was followed by Elliott Automation in 1965 and several others. Rodime of Glenrothes pioneered the 3.5-inch hard disk drive in 1983 and it collected royalties from many manufacturers. The town was well laid out with open spaces and good access from the A92 dual carriageway. It had merged well into the countryside and the other villages and small towns around it.

RIVERSIDE

THE HENGE

GLEN ROTHES

SILICON GLEN

RUBY HENDERSON
JAN MᶜARTHUR
PATRICIA MACINDOE
MAIRI STEWART

THE COO'S TAIL

PANEL 146 The Upper Clyde Shipbuilders

Panel stitched by:

*West of Scotland Guild of
Weavers, Spinners and Dyers*

Susan Black
Margaret Cameron
Alison Christie
Lyn Dunachie
Bron Ellis
Maryel FitzRandolph
Jean Mabon
Liz MacKinlay
Margaret McBlane
Joan McDowall
Christina McLachlan
Marlen McMaster
Katie Shirley
Flora Smith
Caroline Thomson
Mary Wilkinson

Stitched in:
Kilmacolm, Glasgow, Paisley,
Fintry, Johnstone

UCS was formed in 1968 from a group of shipbuilders on the Clyde to become more competitive and achieve economies of scale. But very quickly, in 1971, the company went into receivership after the Conservative government of Edward Heath refused a loan of £6 million. The consortium had a full order book and forecast profits for 1972. Instead of going on strike, the workforce voted to continue working and fulfil the orders. The UCS work-in was led by Jimmy Reid, Jimmy Airlie, Sammy Gilmore and Sammy Barr. All were members of the Communist Party and Reid was a gifted orator. In a speech to the workforce, he emphasised that their demeanour and image were vital. The world was watching and there would be 'no hooliganism . . . no vandalism . . . [and] no bevvying'. The work-in successfully stirred public sympathy, cash was raised and, when John Lennon sent a cheque for £5,000, some wag feigned amazement, saying, 'But Lenin's deid.' In 1972, the government agreed to restructure the yards around two new companies – Govan Shipbuilders and Scotstoun Marine Ltd – and to inject £34 million. It was a victory and shipbuilding continued on the Clyde.

SAVE UCS

Along came a man whose name was Reid
Says he We'll win if we keep the heid

Pack your tools and go
For the yards been sold
The big old gates are closing
The yards are dead
Pack your tools and go

20TH SEPTEMBER 1967

WEST OF SCOTLAND
GUILD
OF
WEAVERS SPINNERS
AND
DYERS

QE2

JOHN BROWN AND CO CLYDEBANK

THERE WILL BE NO BEVVYING

Pack your tools and go
by Jimmie Macgregor

And keep the hammers ringing
Pickup your tools let's go
For hell make our way without their say
Pick up your tools Let's go

UPPER CLYDE SHIPBUILDERS WORK IN, JIMMY REID, 1971

PANEL 147   Stop Yer Ticklin', Jock!

Panel stitched by:

Liz & Marilyn

Barbara Bell
Ursula Doherty
Elizabeth Duke
Tessa Durham
Catherine Jones
Marilyn Nicholson
Dawn White

Stitched in:
Dalkeith, Dunbar

Principally known as a singer and songwriter, Harry Lauder was also very funny. He was the first British artiste to sell a million records and his songs, such as 'Keep Right on to the End of the Road', 'Roamin' in the Gloamin'' and 'A Wee Deoch-an-Doris' are still popular. Lauder came out of the music hall traditions and music has long been associated with Scottish comedy. Perhaps the greatest of Scottish comedians, Billy Connolly, began his performing life with the Humblebums and played the banjo. But there have been other strands. Chic Murray had a surreal brand of humour and Scottish sketch comedy with the likes of Rikki Fulton has been sublime. The Rev. I. M. Jolly is an immortal character. There appears to be such a phenomenon as Scottish humour and what is cheering is that, through the success of Connolly and others, it is understood worldwide.

The Rise of the Scottish National Party

Panel stitched by:

Stitchers Ecosse

Frances Cohen
Ruth Currie
Frances Gardiner
Rhona MacKenzie
Linda Watson

Stitched in:
Longniddry

Arguably the most dynamic force for change in post-war Scottish politics has been the Scottish National Party. It has grown from little more than an irrelevant fringe to become the majority party of government in the new Scottish Parliament. Its rise began with Winnie Ewing's stunning victory at the Hamilton by-election of 1967 and continued with the victories of 11 MPs in the 1974 general election. Ewing has been a central figure in the success of the SNP ever since, winning election after election. Her party forced serious consideration and eventual implementation of Scottish devolution and the resulting Scottish Parliament is now dominated by the SNP. The first referendum on the issue was held in 1979 but hi-jacked by a London Labour MP, George Cunningham. He successfully argued that, if majority of Scots voted yes, then it would have to reach 40 per cent of the electorate. In the event, there was a small majority but it fell short of that percentage. When Labour came to power in 1997, a second referendum was held and the result was an overwhelming majority, 74%, in favour of a Scottish Parliament.

PANEL 149 Scotland at the Movies

Panel stitched by:

Boatie Blest Stitchers

Jackie Berg
John Berg
Carmel Daly
Jon Gerard
Bernie Goslin
Agnes Greig
Marion Harkin
Lucy Hyde
Shelly Jones
Gareth Jones
Jennifer Nesbit
Bill Peach
Martine Robertson
Joyce Souness

Stitched in:
Port Seton

'The name's Bond, James Bond.' Immortal words, uttered by Sean Connery, they established him as one of the most famous film actors of all time. Other Scots, such as Ewan McGregor, Brian Cox, Kelly Macdonald, Tom Conti and Tilda Swinton, have followed. Behind the camera, Alexander MacKendrick, Bill Forsyth and Lynne Ramsay have directed memorable work. And one of the most commercially successful films of all time, *Braveheart*, told the story of a Scottish hero – William Wallace. Definitions can be elusive. Many films have been made in Scotland but can Alfred Hitchcock's wonderful *The 39 Steps* be called a Scottish film? It was adapted from a novel by John Buchan, a Border Scot but directed by an Englishman and had English actors in lead roles. Even Peggy Ashcroft played a crofter's wife. Perhaps one of the very best was *Local Hero*, written and directed by Bill Forsyth in 1983. It starred Americans, Peter Riegert and Burt Lancaster, but also Denis Lawson and Fulton Mackay. But what it portrayed was very Scottish – a Lowlander's use of imagined Highland attitudes to create a modern fairy tale. And, with its superb dialogue and acting and a haunting theme by Mark Knopfler, it was very successful.

SCOTLAND AT THE MOVIES

PANEL 150
Scotland's World Cup in Argentina

Panel stitched by:

Allanwater Stitchers

Ann Gambles
Libby Hughes
Frances Rankin
Catriona Whitton

Stitched in:
Dunblane

Dashed hopes and overblown optimism characterise one of the most calamitous episodes in Scotland's sporting history. Throughout the 1960s and 1970s, Scotland's football team had occasionally been inspired and, when they left for the 1978 World Cup in Argentina, crowds filled Hampden Park and lined the route to Prestwick Airport. They believed they could win the trophy. An opening defeat by Peru made that seem unlikely and a dismal draw against Iran meant that they had to defeat a brilliant Dutch team by three clear goals to avoid going out of the competition. Finally, playing the football of which they were capable, they beat Holland 3–2, with Archie Gemmill scoring one of the greatest goals of all time. From the ridiculous to the sublime, as so often with Scottish sport. At the time of writing, national football languishes in mediocrity, with Scotland ranked 50th in the world, one place below the Cape Verde Islands but above Panama. Fans must sometimes pine for the crazy, heady days of 1978 and marching with Ally's Army.

PANEL 151 The Miners' Strike

Panel stitched by:

Agnes Greig
Pauline O'Brien
Libby O'Brien

Stitched in:
Tranent, Prestonpans

The Miners' Strike of 1984–85 seemed like the end of an era. In the 1970s, the National Union of Mineworkers had humbled a Conservative government but Margaret Thatcher was determined that history would not repeat itself. After stockpiling fuel and deploying police forces all over the country, she succeeded in forcing the miners back to work and pushing through a programme of closure. Secret papers recently released show that she was willing to involve the army in an industrial dispute. Thatcher was fortunate to face Arthur Scargill, a miners' leader who polarised opinion but whose predictions of the demise of deep mining turned out to be accurate. In Scotland, many famous collieries, such as Monktonhall, Bilston Glen, Polmaise, Seafield and Longannet, shut down in the year following the unsuccessful strike. There are no working deep mines left in Scotland and heavy industry has also been drastically reduced. The strike not only changed the face of Scottish industry, it also altered the course of Scottish politics and some would argue not for the better.

MINERS STRIKE 1984
DECLINE OF HEAVY INDUSTRY

PANEL 152 Gaelic Resurgent

Panel stitched by:

Christine Haynes
Pauline Elwell

Stitched in:
Morar

In a very surprising announcement, the Conservative Secretary of State for Scotland, Malcolm Rifkind, announced the creation of a fund to pay for Gaelic television programmes. On 18 December 1989, he outlined a plan to provide £8 million for programmes to be broadcast by the Scottish ITV companies, STV and Grampian. Two hundred hours of new programming was to be commissioned by the Gaelic Television Committee. It proved a massive stimulus and, with the success of the likes of *Machair*, a Gaelic-language soap opera, it put Gaelic back at the centre of Scottish life. At the same time, Gaelic rock music was becoming more and more popular through the phenomenon of Runrig. Formed in Skye, this remarkable band developed a hybrid Gaelic–English form of rock music which often used the narratives of Highland history as its subject matter. The songs were written by the brothers Rory and Calum Macdonald, and the lead singer, Donnie Munro, possessed a sublime voice. Others, such as Capercaillie, were also popular bands. But the twin impact of Gaelic television and Runrig prevented Gaelic from fading from the national agenda. The number of speakers is tiny but there appears to exist a political will to ensure survival of some sort.

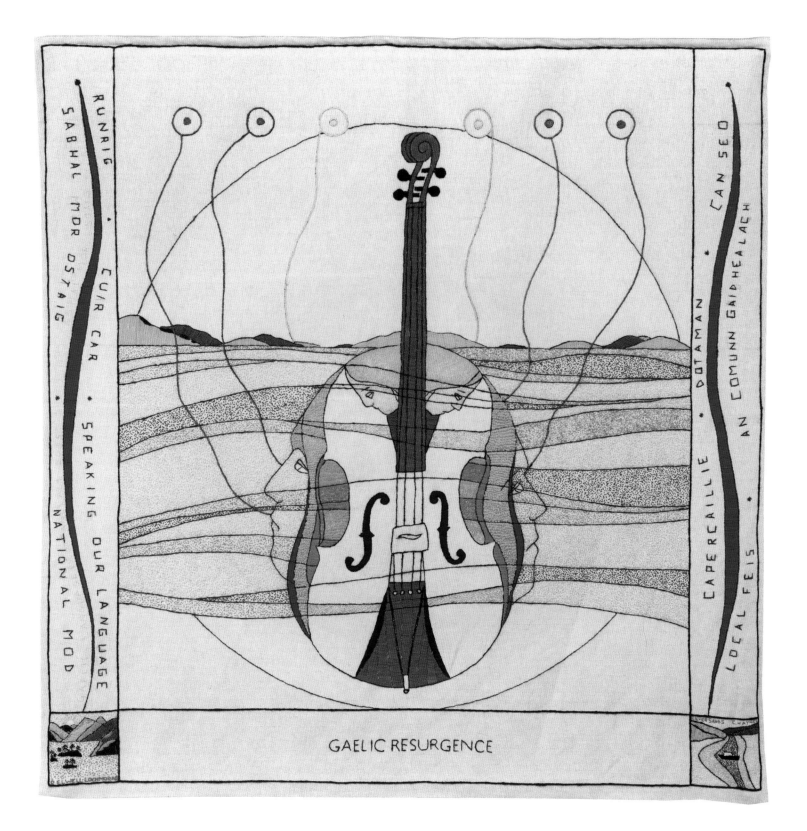

RUNRIG • CUIR CAR • SPEAKING OUR LANGUAGE

SABHAL MÒR OSTAIG • NATIONAL MOD

CAN SEO • DÒTAMAN

AN COMUNN GAIDHEALACH

CAPERCAILLIE • LOCAL FEIS

GAELIC RESURGENCE

PANEL 153 Glasgow – European City of Culture

Panel stitched by:

Fiona Hamilton

Stitched in:
East Renfrewshire

Reinvention lay at the heart of Glasgow's successful bid to become European City of Culture in 1990. An idea formed by the actress Melina Mercouri, the Greek Minister of Culture, and her French counterpart Jack Lang, the intention was to highlight both the diversity and commonality of European culture. Athens, Florence, Amsterdam, Berlin and Paris all preceded Glasgow and all were perhaps more obvious choices. But the old industrial heart of Scotland rose brilliantly to the challenge. All of the city's galleries and theatres took part and some were specially created. At a huge Harland & Wolff engine shed, a play called *The Ship* recalled great industrial traditions. Written by Bill Bryden, it was enormously popular. The celebrations ran for a year and Glasgow capitalised on the exposure to promote itself as a tourist destination.

GLASGOW EUROPEAN CITY OF CULTURE 1990

PANEL 154 Dolly the Sheep

Panel stitched by:

Yvonne Beale

Stitched in:
Orkney

Born in July 1996, Dolly, the first mammal to be cloned, became the world's most famous sheep. At the Roslin Institute near Edinburgh, Ian Wilmut, Keith Campbell and their colleagues succeeded in creating Dolly from an adult somatic cell using the process of nuclear transfer. The donor cell was taken from a mammary gland and the birth of the sheep proved that a cell taken from a specific part of the body could be used to create a complete individual. When Ian Wilmut was asked where the name of Dolly came from her replied, 'Dolly is derived from a mammary gland cell and we couldn't think of a more impressive pair of glands than Dolly Parton's.' Having lived her whole life at the Roslin Institute and given birth to six lambs, Dolly died in 2003. Since she was born, many other large mammals, such as bulls and horses, have been successfully cloned.

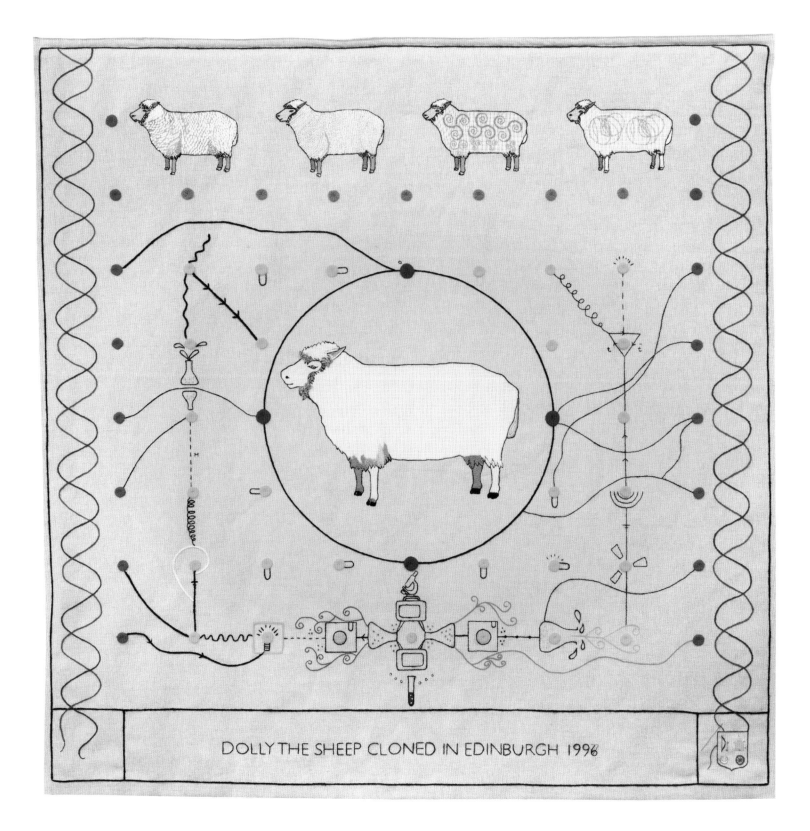

DOLLY THE SHEEP CLONED IN EDINBURGH 1996

The Scottish Parliament Reconvenes, 1999

Panel stitched by:

Scissor Sisters

Linda Jobson
Isobel Reilly
Dorie Wilkie

Stitched in:
Eskbank

When Sheena Wellington sang Robert Burn's great lyric, 'A Man's a Man for A'That' at the opening of the Scottish Parliament in 1999, her beautiful, crystal voice caught the mood of the nation perfectly. All rejoiced on 1 July, Scotland's day. And setting party allegiances aside, all agreed that Winnie Ewing MSP should preside over the opening session. Her memorable words were:

> The Scottish Parliament, adjourned on the 25th day of March in the year 1707, is hereby reconvened.

And despite initial scepticism that Scotland was the most over-governed country in the world and the appalling cost overruns on the construction of the parliament building, the new institution has been a success. It is now difficult to imagine Scotland without MSPs and the debates at Holyrood. No doubt the Scottish Parliament will change, as all vibrant political institutions do, but it is unlikely to disappear as it did in 1707.

THE SCOTTISH PARLIAMENT WHICH ADJOURNED ON 25th MARCH 1707 IS HEREBY RECONVENED

THE SCOTTISH PARLIAMENT RECONVENES 1999

PANEL 156 AND 157
Parliament of the Ancestors, Parliament for the Future

Panel 156 stitched by:

Cupar Needles

Ishbel Duncan
Lisbeth Kervell
Joyce MacRae

Stitched in:
Cupar, Ladybank,
St Andrews

Liberton Ladies

Shirley Dawson
Sheila Farquhar
Dorothy Morrison
Sylvia Robertson
Ann Weir
Margaret Wilson

Stitched in:
Edinburgh

Firth of Forth Stitchers

Sheila Chambers
Celia Mainland
Jenny Mayor
Isabel Weaver

Stitched in:
Prestonpans, Port Seton

Sylvia Robertson

Stitched in:
Pitlochry

Panel 157 stitched by:

Hands Sewlo

Sheila Chambers
Sheena Dolan
Celia Mainland
Jenny Mayor
Isabel Weaver

Stitched in:
Prestonpans, Port Seton,
Edinburgh

Strathmore Stitchers

Doris Black
Nancy Craig
Mary Daun
Valona Gouck
Susan Greaves
Sheila Hawick
Nanette Henderson
Val McDonald
Tessa Mendez
Isobel Ovens
Alison Robertson
Margaret Stanford
Issy Valentine
Irene Ward

Stitched in:
Alyth, Forfar, Letham,
Guthrie, Broughty Ferry

Doreen Scotland
Nan Duffy
Dilly Emslie
Maggie Sturrock
TeresaWallace

Stitched in:
Edinburgh

Sewster Sisters

Annabelle Broadhurst
Alexa Dewar
Catherine Gerrard
Willie Grieve
Fanny Grieve
Jane Jowitt
Irene Martin
Norma McCaskill
Karen Skilling
Elspeth Turner

Stitched in:
Edinburgh, Lasswade

History is about change and change always involves loss. But moments such as the opening of the Scottish Parliament may be seen as a pause and the freeze-frame of a tapestry panel is an attempt to catch that moment and hold it still. The Great Tapestry of Scotland may never end, may be added to over the coming times, but this version pauses with a Parliament of the Ancestors, the men and women who helped make Scotland, and a Parliament for the Future. Two panels show leaders – the four Presiding Officers and the four First Ministers who have held office since 1999. Other living Scots are there and our ancestors below and beside them. They are all flanked by the stitchers – the women who not only made the tapestry but also made a version of Scotland when they first picked up their needles and thread.

CALGACUS
JOHN KNOX
ST COLUMBA
MARY QUEEN OF SCOTS
MARY SOMERVILLE
JOCK STEIN
NORMAN MacLEOD
SAINT NINIAN

CONSTANTINE II · HARRY LAUDER · SOMERLED
MARY SLESSOR
JOHN LOGIE BAIRD
CHARLES RENNIE MACKINTOSH
JENNIE LEE
THOMAS CHALMERS
MALCOLM CANMORE ·
SAINT CUTHBERT
ANDREW CARNEGIE
JOANNA BAILLIE
J.M. BARRIE
LEWIS GRASSIC GIBBON

KIER HARDIE
JOHN WITHERSPOON
ROBERT LOUIS STEVENSON
JEAN ARMOUR
QUEEN VICTORIA
DAVID I ·
ALEXANDER FLEMING
WILLIAM PATERSON
JAMES VI & I
SAINT ANDREW
QUEEN MARGARET · DAVID LIVINGSTONE ·

ROBERT ADAM
JAMES HUTTON
ADAM SMITH
MURIEL SPARK
JOHN NAPIER
LORD REITH

SWRI
JM
ELK
IMMD
SWR
EVELYN STEWART MURRAY

PANEL 156a

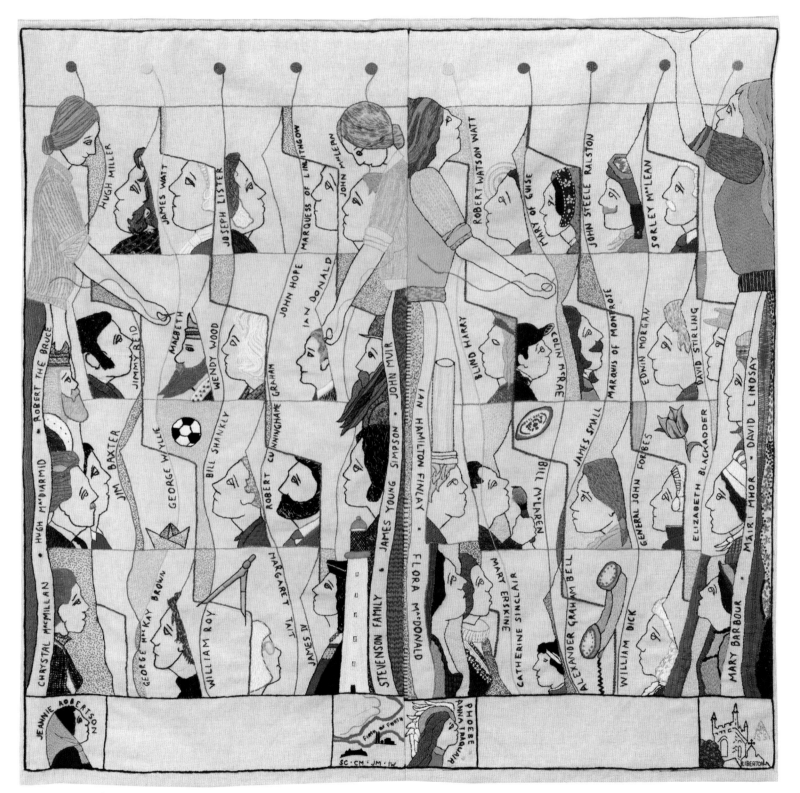

HUGH MILLER
JAMES WATT
JOSEPH LISTER
MARQUESS OF LINLITHGOW
JOHN HOPE
IAN DONALD
JOHN McLEAN
ROBERT WATSON WATT
MARY OF GUISE
JOHN STEELE RALSTON
SORLEY McLEAN

ROBERT THE BRUCE
JIMMY REID
MACBETH
WENDY WOOD
ROBERT CUNNINGHAME GRAHAM
BLIND HARRY
COLIN McRAE
MARQUIS OF MONTROSE
EDWIN MORGAN
DAVID STIRLING

HUGH McDIARMID
JIM BAXTER
GEORGE WYLLIE
BILL SHANKLY
JAMES YOUNG SIMPSON
JOHN MUIR
IAN HAMILTON FINLAY
BILL McLAREN
JAMES SMALL
GENERAL JOHN FORBES
ELIZABETH BLACKADDER
MAIRI MHOR
DAVID LINDSAY

CHRYSTAL McMILLAN
GEORGE McKAY BROWN
WILLIAM ROY
MARGARET TAIT
JAMES IV
STEVENSON FAMILY
FLORA McDONALD
MARY ERSKINE
CATHERINE SINCLAIR
ALEXANDER GRAHAM BELL
WILLIAM DICK
MARY BARBOUR

JEANNIE ROBERTSON

PHOEBE ANNA TRAQUAIR

SC · CM · JM · IW

LIBERTON

PANEL 156b

PARLIAMENT OF THE ANCESTORS

ALEX SALMOND
JACK McCONNELL
HENRY McLEISH
DONALD DEWAR
PROFESSOR DAVID MILNE HOME
JAMES GIBB STUART
STANLEY BAXTER
PAULO NUTINI
THE CORRIES
OOR WULLIE
ALAN WELLS
WINNIE EWING
WALTER SCOTT
ERIC LIDDELL
ELSIE INGLIS
HENRY RAEBURN
MARGOT MacDONALD · THE PROCLAIMERS
ANDY WIGHTMAN
JEAN REDPATH
MAW BROON
HELENA KENNEDY
ANDY MURRAY
SHEENA WELLINGTON
TC SMOUT
JAMES KELMAN
LIZ McCOLGAN

STRATHMORE
STITCHERS

PARLIAMENT FOR THE FUTURE

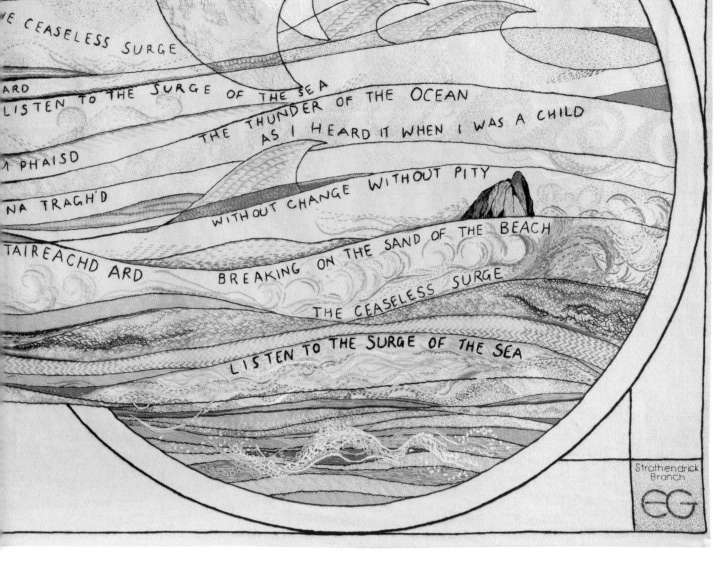

VE CEASELESS SURGE

LISTEN TO THE SURGE OF THE SEA

THE THUNDER OF THE OCEAN
AS I HEARD IT WHEN I WAS A CHILD

ARD

A PHAISD

NA TRAGH'D

WITHOUT CHANGE WITHOUT PITY

TAIREACHD ARD

BREAKING ON THE SAND OF THE BEACH

THE CEASELESS SURGE

LISTEN TO THE SURGE OF THE SEA

Strathendrick Branch

Panel stitched by:

Strathendrick Stitchers

Margaret Burgess
Lyn Dunachie
Margaret Gibb
Margaret Harrison
Christina McLachlan
Moira Murray
Carol Omand
Morag Proven
Susan Rhind
Bette Scott
Marion Tyson
Pam Waller
Heather Wright

Stitched in:
Glasgow, Mingavie,
Fintry, Bearsden,
Drymen, Blanefield,
Killearn

**Panel overleaf
stitched by:**

Meg Porteous

Stitched in:
Edinburgh

PANEL 160